JEANNE HUNT

Holy Bells and Wonderful Smells

Year-Round Activities for Classrooms and Families

To my children—

ALLISON, THOMAS, JONATHAN and CHRISTOPHER—

*who taught me "unless you turn and become like children,
you will not enter the kingdom of heaven" (Matthew 18:3)*

Scripture citations are taken from *The New
American Bible With Revised New Testament*,
copyright ©1986 by the Confraternity of
Christian Doctrine, and are used by permission.
All rights reserved.

Cover and book design by Julie Lonneman
ISBN 0-86716-141-8
Copyright ©1996, Jeanne Hunt
All rights reserved.

Published by St. Anthony Messenger Press
Printed in the U.S.A.

CONTENTS

INTRODUCTION

Symbols, gestures, prayer and ritual are a rich and longstanding part of the Catholic tradition. We need to keep these wonder signs alive in the hearts and faith of all, but especially in the faith life of our children.

The fast pace of our world doesn't make ritual prayer easy. Learning to experience the meaning of a burning fire, the splashing of baptismal water or the smell of holy oil takes a little time. This book offers all of us ways to enter these experiences. We slow down and step into the quiet places of the spirit as we experience the simple prayers of each season.

Take this book into your classrooms, parishes and homes and have fun. Real communion with God should always be filled with joy and playfulness. It is time to rekindle the adventure of ritual in family life and church life.

My experience as a wife and mother, teacher, director of religious education and maker of prayers has fortified me for the task of compiling this almanac of celebration. I have made ritual prayers with jumping toddlers, grieving widows, exhausted mothers and bored teenagers. The fabric of their prayer has been pieced together to make this book. I am the gatherer of the fabric and the sewer of the patches.

This book is meant for the creative and the not-so-creative. You can take a suggestion and add your own style and grace to the ritual or play it by the book. If you have always admired creative types but can't quite muster your own imaginative skills, you'll like this book—all the work has been done for you!

A word of caution: Not every idea is meant for every family or class. Select those ideas that seem to fit your style, spirituality or life circumstances. For instance, when my children were young, I put a basket of straw and an empty manger in our living room one Advent. I directed my toddler crew to put one piece of straw in the manger every time they performed an act of love. Well, my three sons and one daughter loved it for about two days. Then, one of them saw his brother do an act of "unlove," so he took it upon himself to remove a straw from the manger for his brother. The next thing I saw was three boys removing, throwing and stuffing straw all over the living room in the name of "Holy Justice"! It took days to clean up their straw explosion. That Advent project was a real failure for the Hunts, and it has never resurfaced in our family life.

Be flexible; pick and choose your rituals. This book offers a wealth of ideas that span the liturgical and school year. An icon in the margin indicates whether the activity is designed for family, school or both. You don't need to try them all right away. Keep this manual on the shelf and pull it out a few weeks before a season begins. Prayerfully choose one or two projects for this year and save the rest for later. Write in margins and add your own adjustments and suggestions, just as you might alter a recipe.

May this book prime the pump of your own prayerful spirits. Use it with delight. Each page offers a different grace as the seasons change, the saints march on and God meets us along the way.

The
Spirituality

of
Autumn

G od is infinite flare! During autumn we watch a spectacle of color that shouts the style of Yahweh. Orange, red, yellow horizons explode from God's palette and we are enthralled at God's handiwork. We gather at favorite vistas to watch the spectacle and soak in the drama as our Creator dances and splashes color over the earth.

We enter into the energy and excitement of God's movement in this season. By abandoning ourselves to the presence of the Source, we experience God in autumn's color. God laughs all around us. Children recognize this laughter first, but even serious hearts can let go and dance with God. In the autumn landscape God turns laughter from sound to sight. This visual laughter is pure balm for our spirits. God invites us to be drawn into the wonder of color, the laughter, the dance. The simple pleasures of autumn can heal spirits overwhelmed by a world of concrete and glass.

Earth's landscape is varied and splendid. For some, no lush oaks and maples dot the hillsides with red and orange. Instead, the desert tells a more subtle prophecy of the change to winter quiet. Still air turns to sweet moving breezes. Plants return to green winter song as rains bathe the sand. The sun relents and allows the hidden life beneath the crust of rock to emerge. Within the transformation of the desert's autumn we see the Creator painting an image of hope. Life is eternal, even life hidden in the seeds between desert rocks. The days become shorter and night creates darkness and rest.

The autumn of the ocean tells the same tale as water chills and winds change to call the shore into quiet. Marine life journeys to warmth in some distant place. Autumn's song of the sea brings gentle cadence to the tides and the sparkling blues turn to deep green as water and sand are no longer harmonized with the sun's brilliance. In its own way the ocean preaches the quiet of autumn and a walk along the shore calms our spirits in these days.

Autumn offers a more somber note as well. Even as we delight in the joyous color, in the water that comes to the thirsty desert, in the ocean quieting into winter's peace, we realize that the end is near. Soon the earth will lie in a quiet deathlike sleep. In the stark darkness of winter, we find a bittersweet joy. In the changing seasons we know this truth of every life: For every moment of delight and joy, for every birth, we encounter some pain, some sorrow, some death. The balance of this cycle calls us ever deeper into the mystery of our own redemption. Into our pain comes the promise of new and greater life. Even as the earth falls into death, the sweet promise of another spring lies hidden in the dark earth. Jesus invites us into the ageless journey of the paschal mystery. Let us enter into the wonder of the season.

Celebrating Harvesttime

Visit an Apple Farm

Take a class trip or a family outing to a local pick-your-own apple farm. (If you live in an area where apples do not grow, go for a ride into the country with a bag of your favorite apples!) This activity encourages everyone to get outside and enjoy the quiet beauty of God's good earth. Pick several different varieties. Encourage children to taste the difference in various types of apples. When you return home with your supply, make apple pie or another favorite apple treat together. When everyone has finished eating, impress them with your wisdom by saying, "Anyone can count the seeds in an apple, but only God knows how many apples are in a seed!"

Apple Tasting Activity

Hold an apple tasting activity. Let children taste and identify different varieties of apples. You can easily integrate this activity into a science lesson. Explain that God's people are like the many varieties of apples—we have many differences that make us unique, but we all belong to the same basic species. Share with the class this simple analogy: The apple's skin is like God the Parent—it protects the apple from disease and harm; the pulp is like Jesus—it is our nourishment; the seeds are like the Spirit—they hold the promise and hope of growth.

Leaf Saturday

This autumn celebration won't be found on many calendars but is a delightful way to welcome autumn for those who live in climates where the trees change colors. On the Saturday when the leaves are at their autumn brightest take a trip to a nearby park or forest for a visual feast of color. Pick the brightest leaves for your collection as you enjoy a vigorous hike. When you return home, dip your leaves in melted paraffin for a lasting reminder of your day among the trees.

Make leaf cookies for a "Leaf Saturday" dessert. Cut sugar cookie dough in the shape of leaves. When they have baked and cooled, ice them with splotches of red, yellow, orange, brown and green icing. This hands-on activity allows everyone a share in the Artist's handiwork.

Celebrating Leaves

Let the children bring to class the most colorful leaves from home. Discuss the way each leaf is fashioned similarly and yet each leaf has a particular beauty. Point out that God creates a many-splendored variety of both leaves and people. Allow the children to talk about their favorite colors and to describe the colors God gave them: eyes, hair, skin and so on. Write a litany of thanksgiving naming all the colors God has given this class. Use this litany in a prayer service or liturgy during these fall days.

A simple art project will reinforce the lesson of particular beauty. Dip leaves in poster paint and press on absorbent white paper. Vary color and pattern for better effect. Let children create their own designs using the autumn colors they have seen in the leaves. You might add a Scripture verse or a prayer of thanksgiving for creation to these paintings. These colorful paintings bring the wonder of the season into the room and remind us of the love and artistry of our delightful God.

Plant Spring Bulbs

Fall is a time of seeding. Nature produces its birthing pods and buries them deep in the earth's womb, promising that in spring the earth will be visited by tender, new life. This cycle holds abundant lessons. "As we plant, so also shall we reap," says the Lord. Let yourself and those you nurture get in touch with the simple yet profound meaning of nature's process. We are called to plant spiritual, emotional and even physical seeds so that we might know life in abundance.

Purchase a variety of spring bulbs. Compare the different sizes and shapes. Dig holes in the required depths and let the children hide spring's promise in its winter nest. Bury the bulbs with dirt and mulch them with dried leaves.

If you live in a climate where bulbs won't grow or you have limited space, you can do this indoors by burying the bulbs in a large clay pot and covering them with potting soil. Put the pot in a cold, dark place till Ash Wednesday. Then bring the pot into a warm, sunny location. Water, keeping the soil lightly moist. Watch spring unfold in your house or classroom. As the blossoms appear, let your nose soak up the sweet aroma of spring. Easter will be filled with the sign of new life promised in the autumn planting.

When all the bulbs are safely hidden in their winter sanctuary, share cups of hot cider, herbal tea or hot chocolate. Reflect on the passage of time and the ways we plant promises of new life by our actions.

**The Mustard
Seed**

Gather a large collection of seeds. Ask everyone to bring something different to your collection. See how many varieties of pods and seeds you can find. Look at the differences, talk about the wonder of environmental reproduction.

Explore the methods by which seeds are pollinated (this might be integrated with a science lesson). Emphasize how God continues to create new life in the marvelous drama of nature's cycle.

Celebrate the seeds of autumn in a paraliturgy. Read the first creation story in Genesis (1:1—2:4). Then ask children to come forward one by one with their favorite seeds. Let them describe their seeds as they place them before a lighted candle.

After each seed is presented, the leader says, "For this promise of life and hope of creation, we say," and everyone answers, "We thank you, Lord."

Then read together the parable of the mustard seed (Matthew 13:31-32). Remind children of the large plants promised in these seeds and of their own potential as they grow. Close with this prayer:

> God of everything created,
> bless and prosper our earth.
> Teach us to care for every seed you send.
> May these little seeds we hold in our hands
> be signs of hope, signs of wonder for us.
> May we never forget your care and love for us.

Celebrating the Beginning of School

Autumn brings to a sudden halt the laziness of summer days. As classrooms reopen their doors and families go back into high gear, we look at these last days of summer as a source of consolation and enjoyment. Family, school and church activities begin anew. As bathing suits and beach towels give way to sweatshirts and soccer balls, we look to autumn as a time to reenter life, to get involved again after the summer sabbatical. Whether you are called to motivate the "child of summer" in your classroom or rejuvenate the family spirit after the dog days of August, these activities will spark everyone's interest.

**School
Supplies
Activity**
♥

Set aside a time to go shopping for all those erasers and glue bottles that your students need. While some children love to get ready for the first day of school, others dread it. Turn the preparation time into a positive experience for everyone. After the shopping is complete, take some time together over pizza or a sundae to talk about the good things that happen as we return to school. Reassure your children that getting back into the discipline of school life isn't easy, but it is an important part of growing into adulthood. Be there to listen to their fears and offer support as they spend this time with you.

**Gifts for the
Teacher**
♥

Students throughout the world start school at this time. In Russia students bring their teachers flowers. In Burma the traditional gift on the first day of school is a coconut or banana. Help your children think of simple, creative gifts for their teachers at the beginning of the school year.

**Home From
the First Day
of School**
♥

Plan a special after-school snack to greet your tired students as they come home. If you are working parents and your children come home to an empty house, prepare a little surprise: Write a little love note, promising some special time when everyone comes together at the end of your working day.

Listen to their tales of woe and joy. Be sure to ask the classic questions: "Where is your desk?" "Who is your teacher?" "Did everyone return this year?" "Are there any new people?" "What is your favorite class going to be?" When you finish this time together, give each of your children the kind of hug God gives us to show divine delight in all we do. Remember that you are God's arms for your child.

**Pack a
Learning
Lunch**
♥

The same old brown bag with the regular fare gets boring and dull after the first week or two. Try offering a "food of the week" theme. For example, you might use apples to make apples and caramel dip, applesauce and apple-and-cheese kabobs. You can do something similar with nuts, veggies, potatoes and so on.

Another way to perk up school lunches is to include an occasional little surprise in the lunchbox, a sprinkling of love. Like the fast food restaurant kids' meals, include a new eraser, a funny joke, a bookmark.

You might decorate a plain brown bag with a colorful sticker and a current events question from the morning paper. The question can be answered at the evening supper table as the opening topic of conversation.

A 'Here We Are!' Celebration

A new teacher, new schedules, perhaps even a new school, can make the beginning of school tense and difficult. New shoes, new faces, new clothes change the texture of the day. Ease the adjustment by having a "Here we are!" celebration.

Ask each student to interview another student (preferably someone they do not know well) by asking five "favorite" questions such as:

> What is your favorite color?
> What is your favorite food?
> What is your favorite sport?
> What was your favorite vacation?
> What is your favorite song?

Have each student introduce the person interviewed by telling the class some of those favorites. After this experience spend some time in prayer giving thanks for one another. You may wish to plan a prayer service to conclude this time. Older students could plan this closing rite themselves.

Posters About Us

Ask students to make posters about themselves. Include photographs, vital statistics and lots of other favorites such as hobbies, talents, great trips. Hang these posters around the classroom. During the first few weeks of school ask one or two students each day to explain their posters, perhaps during religion class.

These simple exercises build community and ownership in your classroom. As each person tells his or her story, a bond begins to form among students. They become a unique group. The "fifth grade class" is no longer a nondescript group. They become a blend of favorites and gifts like no other before them. Conclude these introductory classes by selecting a class symbol or name like "Mrs. Morgan's Marvelous Marauders."

Celebrating Halloween (October 31)

Halloween's roots lie in an ancient pagan festival for the dead. While this autumn feast can be used for evil purposes, our culture celebrates it as an innocent night of begging and fun. We who believe in the Light of the world can use it to celebrate the Light. "Hallow" means holy and the word *Halloween* refers to the night before the feast of all holies, or All Saints' Day. Emphasize all things good, joyful and pure. Let your children know that they are "children of the Light" called to walk in the Light.

Costume Box

Get a head start on Halloween preparations by spending an afternoon gathering dress-up goodies for your trick-or-treaters. Put old, funny-looking clothing, wigs, makeup, whatever you find in a box. On the day of Halloween get out your box and let children create their own characters. Encourage them to be funny and outrageous.

Halloween Party

As an alternative to letting your children go begging, try hosting a party for your children and their friends. Give each child an empty bag. Let the party goers earn their treats by performing nice tricks for the adults. Be sure to provide lots of nutritious snacks for the bags as well as a few sweet surprises. Carve pumpkins, bob for apples, have a bonfire, enjoy the beauty of the autumn night without worrying about your children's safety.

Family Saints

Since this is the night before All Saints' Day, it is a great idea to explore the family saints. Let your children find out who their patron saints are and why they are so honored. They may even choose to dress up like Saint Joan of Arc, Saint George the Dragon Slayer or Saint Francis of Assisi. They could have fun letting their friends guess who they are by giving clues about their saint's life...for a treat of course!

Pumpkin Farm Visit

Take a trip to a pumpkin farm or country market to pick out the family pumpkin. Take along a loaf of pumpkin bread (see recipe following) and a jug of apple cider. When you get home with the family pumpkin(s), ask everyone to draw faces on paper. Let the family vote on the winning face(s) before the carving begins.

Pumpkin Bread

1-2/3 cup flour	2 eggs
1-1/4 cup sugar	1/2 cup vegetable oil
1 teaspoon baking soda	1/3 cup water (or less)
1/2 teaspoon cinnamon	1/2 cup chopped nuts
1/2 teaspoon nutmeg	1 cup pumpkin
1/4 teaspoon salt	

Mix dry ingredients; add nuts. Mix in egg, oil, water and pumpkin. Stir until blended. Bake in a greased loaf pan (9" x 5" or 10" x 4") 60 to 70 minutes in a 350-degree oven.

Candle Blessing
🍎

Whenever an opportunity arises to combine the sacred and the secular to enrich your students' faith, take advantage of it. Halloween provides just such an opportunity. Children have horrible, unspoken fears about "things that go bump in the night." This occasion is a perfect time to teach the simple gospel truth that the Light does indeed outshine the darkness.

Ask each child to bring a candle to class. Clean out the inside of a large pumpkin. Carve a smiling face on the pumpkin. Talk about the joy of laughing together. Tell students that smiles, laughter and joy are simple gifts that God gives us to erase sadness and fear. Ask them how they feel when they see a scary pumpkin. How do they feel when they look at this smiling one? Decide together which one is the most like God. Then share with the class the wonder that each of us has within us the power to be a light just like Jesus. We become a light that can erase hatred, evil, pain and sadness. The light in us is just like Jesus' light. Put a large candle in your smiling jack-o-lantern. Darken the room if possible. Watch the flame as it fills the pumpkin and lights the room. Notice how much more intense the smile becomes with the light shining through. Ask children to hold their candles in front of them while you say this blessing:

God who created pumpkins and people,
bless our beautiful Halloween light.
This light reminds us that Jesus is the light of the world.
Jesus shines through the darkness
and turns the night into day,
sadness into joy,
hate into love

and tears into smiles.
Bless the candles that we hold.
Let them be a reminder that we are your candles
lighting up the smiles and hearts of our friends and family.
Bless the happy pumpkins we will carve for our candles,
that everyone who sees them might never be afraid of the
    darkness
because your wonderful Light is with us.

You might close this prayer service with a rendition of "This Little Light of Mine" or another hymn about light.

All Saints'
Festival
🍎

Another enjoyable exercise for the school setting is to hold an All Saints' festival for children and their families on the occasion of Halloween. Each class designs a fund-raising booth for the festival. Activities such as a ring toss, a fishing pond, "guess your weight" and so on are typical of this festival. The money raised could be sent to a favorite mission or charity. Conclude the festival with an outdoor parade in which all students dress up like their favorite saints and "parade" around the school neighborhood.

Celebrating Thanksgiving

Thanksgiving originated at a time when the spiritual dimension of life was an integral part of people's lives. Eighteenth-century Puritan society was centered in a deep, abiding faith in God. These "pilgrim people" of America found it natural to give thanks to God for all their blessings.

    Thanksgiving still offers a great opportunity to reflect on all that God has done for us and to give thanks to God in recognition of that goodness and providence. On Thanksgiving we integrate the great blessings of our lives with the source of life, our Creator. We can take an ordinary "Turkey Day" and weave a simple message of the sacred throughout the celebration.

The Five
Kernels of
Corn
⌂ 🍎

Shortly before Thanksgiving, plan a meal for the class or for family and friends. Share the story of the first Thanksgiving. The first year the Pilgrims spent in America was bleak and morbid. Starvation loomed over their heads like earth's greatest darkness. The daily ration throughout that first winter is said to have been five kernels of corn per meal. It is no wonder that their hearts were so grateful at the second year's bountiful harvest.

Invite your guests to the table, which has been decorated for a feast. Before you bring the food to the table, bring to each hungry diner a plate with five kernels of corn (use canned or frozen corn). Let everyone eat their portions, then ask if they feel satisfied with the "meal." Discuss the empty feeling after such a meager meal.

Expand the discussion to include questions such as these: What would we do if there were no more food? What might real hunger feel like? Where in our world, our country, our city do families leave their table hungry? Show some photographs of the victims of hunger. Conclude by reflecting on the bounty we have.

After the experience of hunger has settled in their souls, serve a simple meal to your guests. As they share the meal, ask again how they feel. End this meal with a mutual prayer of Thanksgiving. Ask each person for a brief prayer of gratitude, such as, "For the hands that prepared this food...." Ask everyone to respond, "We thank you, Lord."

If you are doing this activity in the classroom, you might plan a simple project to conclude your meal. Cut a 4" x 4" square of colored netting. Put five kernels of unpopped popcorn in the middle and tie with colored yarn or ribbon. Let the children each make enough for the guests at their family Thanksgiving meal. Instruct the children to place these party favors on each guest's empty plate before the family feast begins and share the story of the first winter in Plymouth with their guests.

Sharing the Bounty

• Provide a complete Thanksgiving meal for a needy family. If you are aware of a family that is unable to prepare the meal, cook and deliver a meal for them before your own feast.

• Collect canned goods and nonperishable items and take them to a local shelter for the homeless.

• Spend Thanksgiving Day working in a soup kitchen. The experience of giving away your time and energy on this feast will provide "food" for your spirit.

• A geography class might want to adopt a missionary church in a Third World country. Use a map of a country to locate the mission. Your diocesan mission office will be happy to supply you with a contact in the mission church. Write to the pastor or coordinator and ask what your class could do for them. Work with all your energy to fulfill their request and pray for your special people every day. Send your donations around the time of Thanksgiving and continue to serve this mission community throughout the remainder of the year.

Fasting Before the Feast

In the days before Thanksgiving set aside one day to fast. Plan your "famine" for a day when everyone can participate. Agree on some way as a family to deny yourselves for this one day. For example, each person could eat only a bowl of rice for dinner. Before you eat this meal offer a prayer for those who are dying of starvation. Let it be a day of reflection and prayer for those without the food gifts we take for granted.

You might want to invite a group of families to join you in this effort. On the designated day, each family can abstain and fast during the day and then gather in the evening for a simple shared meal, perhaps a meatless soup with bread. Allow the group to savor this time and share their reflections of their fasting day. End the evening with prayer. Invite each family to contribute to the prayer time with prayers of thanksgiving, readings from Scripture, stories from their own family history of days of plenty and days of want, and so on.

In the classroom this planned famine could be a lunchtime experience. Study what children in Third World countries eat for their lunch (or, more realistically, for their one daily meal!). Serve this menu in the school cafeteria. It might consist of rice and water, or thin chicken broth with a few sliced carrots. After the meal is served, pass a basket to collect the money the students usually spend on dessert and snacks. Send this contribution to your school's favorite mission project.

Giving Thanks

Thanksgiving is a good time for people to verbalize what they're thankful for. Classes could do this on the last day of school before Thanksgiving; families could do this as they gather around "the bird." Invite everyone to name something they're most thankful for. The answers may surprise people, make them think and add to the prayerfulness of the celebration.

Celebrating Other Autumn Feasts

National Hispanic Heritage Month
(September 15-October 15)

Our Catholic Church in the Americas has a large percentage of Spanish-speaking members. This month is a great time to learn a little more about the foods of our Hispanic culture. Have a Mexican buffet during this month. Two books that offer good recipes are: *De Grazia and Mexican Cookery* (*Arizona Highways*, 2039 West Lewis Ave., Phoenix, AZ 85009) and *Mexican Cookbook: Sunset Series* (Lane Books, 80 Willow Road, Menlo Park, CA 94025).

Rosh Hashanah
(late September)

Discover the meaning of the Jewish New Year. Research the customs of this Jewish holiday such as the *shofar* (ram's horn). A class could invite a local rabbi or Jewish parent to share and demonstrate the Hebrew rituals of this holiday.

Sukkot
(mid-October)

The Jewish Feast of Sukkot or Tabernacles celebrates God's divine providence throughout the journey of life. The date for this feast varies according to the Jewish calendar. Find out when it is celebrated this year. Make a centerpiece out of small twigs, leaves, wheat and nuts to symbolize God's continuing presence through the years and cycles of life.

National American Indian Heritage Month
(November)

Let students research the ways of Native American prayer. Plan a prayer service reverencing the earth in honor of the Native American culture using traditional symbols of cornmeal, fire and plants. Learn which Native Americans are native to your area. Listen to a recording of traditional Native American music.

Native American Prayer Service

Preparation: Place a bowl of cornmeal, a houseplant and a candle on your prayer table. Find a small drum.

Begin by sitting in a circle around the prayer table. One person slowly beats the drum while another lights the candle.

Reader 1: Maker of the earth,
trees, animals and humans,

all is for your glory.
The drum beats it out
and the human beings shout it;
they dance the ancient dance
that says you are God.

The drum stops. One person stands, takes the bowl of
cornmeal and throws a little cornmeal first to the north, then
to east, south and west in turn. The following prayers can be
read between compass points or at the end of the cornmeal
ritual.

Reader 2: O Great Spirit of the North,
we ask you for strength and power
to be strong and sure
when the cold uncertain wind
wants to blow us away.

O Great Spirit of the East,
we smile at you when the sun comes up.
Give light to our ways,
especially to those who will be born today.

O Great Spirit of the South,
whose warmth brings growth to our seeds,
help us to grow in your ways.

O Great Spirit of the West,
where each night the sun comes to rest,
bless us with peace.

All children stand.

Reader 3: Trees and living things
are one in your life.
We thank you for giving us the earth
and all its plants and animals.
We promise to care for them.

The drum begins to beat again very slowly. Everyone bows
toward the prayer table and stays in a position of reverence
until the drum stops.

September 22
Farewell-to-Summer Picnic

September 22 is the last day of summer. Celebrate the close of the season with a farewell picnic. Serve lemonade, Popsicles and typical summer fare. Get a large box and let everyone fill it with the things you won't be using till next June: suntan lotion, beach toys, flip-flops.... Toss water balloons or run through a lawn sprinkler. Say goodnight to summer by catching the last fireflies or picking the last blooms from the garden or looking at summer vacation photos or whatever says "It's over" for you. Offer a family prayer of thanksgiving for the summer you have just shared.

Good-bye-to-Summer Prayer

Creator God,
as the last summer sun folds into the horizon,
we thank you for being our companion in this season.
Was it you we heard laughing as we splashed in cool waters?
Was it you who made the sweet smell of newly mown grass?
Was it you twinkling a smile in the night stars?
Yes! Oh yes! It was you!
We are grateful, God, that you took time
to journey through summer with us.
As the night bleeds into autumn,
we await the surprise of your next step. Amen.

October 4
Feast of Saint Francis of Assisi

This saint showed his love of creation through his tender care for God's creatures. Bless pets or ask children to bring photos of their pets to school.

Francis had a great love for the environment and his mission was always to the poor. Make a bird treat by spreading peanut butter on pinecones and rolling them in birdseed. Hang these gooey gifts in your favorite tree and watch the local feathered friends gather.

Share one of the amazing folktales that surround the life of Francis. Say the "Peace Prayer" attributed to Saint Francis as a fitting closure to time spent with this special saint.

October 9
**Death of
Benjamin
Banneker**

Benjamin Banneker was born in 1736. He was known as the first black man of science. He was a surveyor, scientist and astronomer. He wrote an almanac and was noted in his time as a true scholar, although he had to fight against a presumption that black people were not as intelligent as white people. This is a great day to spend time thinking about subtle discrimination that lies in the corners of our hearts.

Make a "Dust Balls in the Corner" list of your negative feelings about people who are different from you (poor people, old people, fat people, people who wear glasses, people with disabilities, and so on). Ask God to forgive and heal you of such discrimination. Then sweep the dust balls out of the corners of your heart! Make a tiny broom out of toothpick and yellow paper bristles and put it in a prominent place to remind you to keep sweeping the dust balls out of your heart.

November 9
**Birthday of
Dorothy Day**

In the first half of this century Dorothy Day founded the Catholic Worker Movement through which she provided hospitality homes for the poor and homeless. In honor of this modern-day holy woman hold a Dorothy Day Canned Food Drive. Take your offerings to a local center for the homeless.

Dirty Room Week

In honor of Dorothy Day plan a "Dirty Room Week" to bring the class to a greater awareness of their own wealth and others' needs and to help them understand the gospel message in their own terms.

Ask children to clean their rooms this week (with a parent's help and approval). Tell them to go through closets, drawers, desks and collect any usable toys and clothes to be given to the poor. Ask parents to sign a "Job Well Done" form and a release form for the objects the child wishes to donate. On the designated day, bring the items to class. Invite a member of a local charitable organization to accept your offering and share with the class the work that the organization does and the great need that exists in the community.

Close the week of effort with the following prayer based on the beatitudes. Prepare a prayer table with a cross and candle.

Prayer for the Poor

Hungry, tired, cold and poor Jesus,
I want to see you in my world.
My world of comfort and full refrigerators
   and shopping malls.
I know where you are, Jesus.
You are with the poor.

Light the candle.

You are standing with the twelve-year-old boy
who is ashamed to go to school
because his clothes are dirty and torn.
Help me to offer him clothes.

Put an article of clothing on the table.

You are standing with the single mom
who lives in an apartment without heat or electricity.
Help me pay her bill.

Put money on the table.

You are standing with the homeless man
who has not eaten in days.
Help me to feed him.

Put canned goods on the table.

You are standing with a lonely, sick, old woman
who can no longer leave her house
because of fear and illness.
Help me to ease her pain.

Put a flower on the table.

Jesus, show us the way
to change our hearts
with actions and love. Amen.

November 15
The Feast of
Shichi-Go-San

On this day in Japan children go to the shrines and pray for good health and fortune. This is a great day to celebrate the child within each of us. Play a game, eat an ice cream cone, read a classic children's story. As a special treat on the feast of Shichi-Go-San, create your own fortune cookies. Put small expressions of good luck or hope for the future inside cone-shaped salty treats or tie your fortunes to a cookie.

The SPIRITUALITY

# of WINTER

When the earth begins to sing of death, our hearts sense the stillness and we feel anxious about what is coming. Winter brings a time of deep quiet to life. Those who have lived long and well know there is nothing to fear in death. In this barren time, life is at rest. We learn that the earth and those who live on it need a time of stillness for birth to occur. For us to join nature in this stillness takes the grace of courage. As we settle into a winter pace, God's quiet searching voice can be heard. It is an Advent voice that speaks the hard truth calling us to turn around and prepare the way for a birth.

Advent calls us to be listeners, to hear our own spirit's longing and the response of a loving God. This exchange occurs in darkness, where nothing can distract us from the sound and sight of God moving in our midst. Just as Mary spoke her fiat with no understanding of what was to come, so too do we open our lives to the unknown ways of the encounter with Christ. The mystery of God among us still remains. In this dark winter solstice the presence of the incarnate word begins, not as a blast of Easter trumpets, but as a small, singular note that is first heard in the birth cry of a winter night.

We are invited to be still and relish the Advent quiet. We learn that darkness is holy and that the night is a time for rejuvenating rest. All this is part of God's way for the earth and for its people. The natural cycle of the seasons speaks to the spiritual cycle of our lives. All parts of the country experience this time of winter rest even where the weather is not cold. The subtle changes of climate, the hibernation of plants and animals set the mood of rest and darkness. The paradox remains with us, that in the stillness comes the promise of future life. The invitation to walk into the silent rest of this season is always an invitation into growth and hope. Winter's song is filled with promise and wonder.

Celebrating Advent

In our consumer world Christmas begins about a month before Thanksgiving. Christmas decorations, caroling bells, twinkle-toed elves appear well in advance of the feast, so that shoppers will shop, spenders will spend and profits will rise. Overwhelmed with the Christmas pitch, we find minimal public awareness of this waiting time called Advent.

Advent shines as the time of expectation. These four weeks before the celebrated birth feast are meant to symbolize centuries of yearning for the Messiah. Advent calls believers to rediscover the reasons for our belief in Jesus as the Christ. It is a season meant to encourage a personal and profound interior journey of waiting, a season modeled on the pregnant virgin's journey to birth. Mary stands as a solitary figure of courageous hope in the midst of darkness. Mary, the human being, simply said, "Yes!"

It is our task to retrieve this quiet season for our hearts and homes. Without walking into the loneliness of the wait, the word Emmanuel, "God with us," has little meaning. Children can rediscover the wealth of Advent traditions that turn their eyes away from television commercials for the latest toy fads and back to Jesus and the values of his gospel. The following suggestions for the season of Advent will keep young and old eyes centered on Jesus, the long-awaited Messiah.

The Advent Wreath

A symbol central to our waiting time should be the Advent wreath. Classrooms, homes and churches offer this symbol as a sign of the journey to Christmas. Traditionally, the wreath is made of evergreens, which represent the constant and eternal presence of God made manifest in Jesus Christ. The wreath is circular, reminding us that God's love is never ending. Four candles are placed on the wreath to symbolize the four Sundays before Christmas. Since the liturgical color of the season is purple, three candles are purple (or white with purple ribbons attached). A fourth candle, to be lit on the third Sunday of Advent, can be pink (or white with a pink ribbon), as a sign to revel in the joy of the nearness of the feast. A fifth candle, white, known as the Christ candle, may be placed in the center of the wreath and lit on Christmas day.

Each Sunday of Advent, a new candle is lit and a simple prayer is said. You may want to read the Gospel or responsorial psalm from that day's liturgy. Families may want to begin a daily meal in these Advent weeks with a special prayer as they light their wreath. Morning prayer in the classroom can feature this ritual throughout the Advent period. *Catholic Household Blessings and Prayers*, published by the U.S. Catholic Conference, offers simple Advent prayers.

Advent wreaths do not have to include evergreens. Here are some interesting variations:

The John the Baptist Wreath

Fill a clay saucer or deep tray with sand (kitty litter is a good substitute if you do not live with a cat!). Place two or three rocks in the pot. Then make a miniature banner that reads "Prepare the

Way of the Lord"; attach it to a small stick and place it in the pot. Place four candles in the sand.

This desert wreath reminds us of the Baptist's cry and suggests what life would be like without the water of life found in Jesus. If you live near the desert, this is a great time to visit the winter desert and recreate it in your Advent desert garden. You might arrange other desert objects such as cactus and bones to illustrate this theme. This little desert place can entice children's imaginations and teach young and old alike to focus on water as the source of life.

In the days before Christmas, wet the sand and add evergreens to the "desert." Talk about the difference in sight, touch and smell between the sand and the evergreens. Remind children that Jesus makes our spirits come alive just like water brings life to the desert. On Christmas Day, add a red bow as a symbol of God's love and a large white candle as a sign of Christ. With older children, you can add small shiny glass ornaments as a symbol of the light of Christ.

As you light the candles of your wreath on Christmas, say this prayer:

> God, may we be like shining ornaments
> reflecting the light of Jesus.
> May our lives mirror his love and his ways,
> not only this Christmas Day, but every day.

During the octave of Christmas, continue to light this centerpiece. Everyone can add ornaments for the times they reflected the love and light of Jesus by their actions. This activity is perfect for those back-to-school days after Christmas. Adding ornaments reminds students that for the Church Christmas continues well into January.

A Bread Dough Wreath

This miniature Advent wreath is a great classroom activity. Make a small wreath of braided bread dough or any type of modeling clay and add four small birthday candles. Let the wreath dry to hardness. Then paint the wreath with bright green paint. These small wreaths can be taken home as reminders of the passing days of Advent.

The Advent Chain

Make a paper chain to count the days before Christmas. As children remove links and the chain grows shorter, they can measure the nearness of the feast. An interesting twist to this project that attracts even the most sophisticated teen is the addition of a task written on the inside of each paper link. These tasks can be little things the family or class does to prepare for the feast. The tasks should be a mixture of physical and spiritual fun activities and caring activities. For instance, "Offer the birds a message of hope today. Feed them a piece of bread or some seed"; "Send a Christmas card to a lonely person" and so on. This chain not only marks the days but prepares our hearts for Christmas.

The Advent House

Getting Christmas decorations out of storage and putting them up can be a great hassle for busy people. Here is an alternative for keeping the spirit of Advent in mind. On the First Sunday of Advent, put out just one small knickknack or wreath. Then each day of Advent add one more decoration. As Christmas approaches, put up the more flamboyant items such as door wreaths and pine boughs. Let everyone guess what decoration was added that day. As the house begins to sparkle with holiday signs, it will be harder to discover what could be new each day. Your space becomes a visual Advent calendar, and by Christmas the decorations are all in place without devoting hours to the effort.

In the classroom, this activity can keep students present to the academic space in a time when their pre-Christmas minds tend to wander. Each day of Advent the class could add something seasonal to the room: a poster, a prayer, a sprig of holly. Enjoy children's reactions as they discover the subtle placement of the new decoration. You might use each day's symbol as the introduction to the day's religion class. You could use Jesse tree symbols as a theme or create an alphabet of Advent symbols: A is for Advent wreath, B is for baby, C is for candle, etc.

The Faces of Jesus

In these days when we await Christ's coming, we might think about the many faces of Jesus Christ. Create a collage of pictures showing the races and cultures that show us the many faces of Jesus Christ among us today. Encourage students to watch for Christ in the faces of the people they meet. Add to your collage throughout Advent.

Christ Kindl

Christ Kindl is a wonderful German tradition that teaches the spirit of giving in the finest gospel sense. Have everyone select the name of another member of the family or class through a secret drawing. Remind them to keep their *Christ Kindl*'s name to themselves till Christmas Eve. All through the days of Advent, they do unseen favors for their *Christ Kindl* as they would for the Christ Child: Hang up a coat, shine shoes, leave a Christmas cookie on a lunch plate, be thoughtful and caring in quiet ways, anything that shows love. On Christmas Eve (or the last day of school before the Eve) they reveal the identity of their *Christ Kindl*. This emphasizes the real experience of giving: not an exchange of material things, but rather gifts from a caring heart.

This project is as successful with adult groups as with families and children. It becomes a great challenge to leave thoughtful notes in your person's mail box, have a favorite pizza delivered on a Friday night, send a favorite book—all without being discovered.

The spirit of giving can take on a particular focus by adopting a needy family. You can find such a family by contacting a local social service agency or simply by keeping your ears and eyes open to those around you. A parish family suddenly overwhelmed by unemployment, illness or death would be perfect for this activity. In a *Christ Kindl* spirit, prepare a cache of Christmas gifts for your family, a Christmas supper, or whatever they need most. You can let them know ahead of time or simply leave your gifts at their door and ring the doorbell, whichever is more appropriate.

Adopting needing families is a wonderful class project. Connecting with other children in need brings the spirit of Christmas into focus and balances the more material aspects of the holiday, helping the students achieve a proper perspective.

The Advent Game

This waiting game spans many age groups and settings. It has been used in classrooms, families, prayer groups and whole parish communities. More than a game, it is a journey into Christmas with the Holy Spirit, who enters into the play of holiness with us. Laughter and inspiration accompany this game as participants meet the joyful side of God in the works of the Spirit. It reminds us to savor the moments of Advent and prepare our hearts for the holy antics of an unpredictable God.

To play the Advent Game, find a basket, empty cookie jar or another container. Then reproduce (rewrite, type or copy) the

Advent activities that follow these directions. The first list is for family use and the second for classroom use. Personalize the activities in any ways that seem appropriate. The Spirit may have some particular ideas for your situations. Cut apart the activities, fold each and place all in the container.

On the first day of Advent, as you choose a piece of paper from the container, ask the Holy Spirit to help you draw closer to God this season. Try to perform your special daily task with a holy purpose and great determination! If you realize that the activity you have drawn is "just impossible" for this day, put it back, remind the Spirit of your schedule and choose again.

Family Advent Activities

• Read the Magnificat today (Luke 1:46-55). Read the words as if Mary is sharing her thoughts and spirit with you in this ancient prayer. Keep the spirit of Mary with you throughout the day by keeping a symbol of her presence visible all day: a lighted blue candle at your table, a rosary in your pocket or some other reminder.

• Wish your nose a "Merry Christmas" today. Prepare a saucepan of two cups of water, a cinnamon stick, orange peels, cloves and nutmeg. Let this mixture simmer on a low heat all day. Add water as necessary. As the sweet aroma fills your house, let it be a sensate prayer of praise that rises to a God who so loved the world that we received the only begotten Son.

• Write letters today to people faraway who touched your life in a special way. Let them know that the memory of your relationship is still with you and that you will always be grateful for their role in your life. Wish them a blessed feast and let them know you will be thinking of them and praying for them this Christmas. Spend the rest of this day praying for these special people.

• Bake your favorite cookies today. (If you're not a cook, visit your favorite bakery.) Freeze these scrumptious treats leaving out two cookies for each family member. In late afternoon or after supper serve these cookies with your favorite hot drink. As you enjoy your treats talk about your expectations for the season. What is your favorite part of the feast? With whom would you like to share it? What silly thing do you always love doing together?

• Go to a shopping mall today. Sit in the midst of the holiday rush and watch the crowd. As you watch the passing shoppers, ask the Spirit to help you single out one overworked, overtired person to pray for. Put something on your refrigerator that will remind you to pray for this person throughout Advent, asking God's blessings, love and peace this Christmas. Picture this person in your mind as you pray. Your prayers may be the greatest gift the person receives this Christmas.

• Listen to Christmas music today. Pray the words as you listen. Let the words melt into your spirit and stay with you throughout the day.

• Invite a lonely neighbor or relative to your home during the week between Christmas Day and New Year's Day. Share the warmth and love of your home with someone who will be without these graced gifts during the feast. Plan a special menu, present a token gift. Attend to this project as if you were inviting Christ for dinner. Meditate today on these words: "Whatever you do for the least among you, you do for me."

• Take a "me" break today. Remember that you are the beloved of God. How will this gracious lover treat you today? Is there something special you would enjoy today—a walk in the quiet morning, a phone call to a distant friend, a leisurely afternoon nap? Let the Spirit treat you to a break in the hectic preparations. Realize that you need to pamper yourself a little so that you don't forget how loved you really are.

• Go for a ride tonight and view all the colorful Christmas lights. Get caught up in the wonder and delight of the spectacle. See it as if you have never viewed such wonder before. Allow the lights to shine in your soul. Feel the joyful glory they proclaim. Allow the Light to brighten your own personal darkness tonight. As you get lost in the vision of colored lights, give back to God any pain or hurt you harbor in your heart.

• Eat lunch today with a good friend. Enjoy this friendship as you break bread together. Remember to thank this special friend for all the relationship means to you. Bring a small gift if you wish, but mostly, just enjoy this dear one. Ask God to keep your friend well this Christmas.

• Think of someone who could use a little boost from God today. Prepare a small and thoughtful gift for this person. Wrap your offering and attach a note that simply says "The Lord made me think of you today." Don't sign it. Let your person feel amazed without any honor for yourself.

• Proclaim a desert day! Fast from noise today. Spend this day quietly in the house—no television, no radio, no telephone calls going out. Keep a deep peace in the house. Spend some extra time listening to God's voice in this quiet day. Let the Spirit speak to you about the weeks ahead and God's ways for the feast in your lives. Write down a few of these thoughts. Keep this journal in the place where you pray and remind yourself of this time of oasis and sanctuary amidst the clamor of holiday noise.

• Prepare a box of food for the poor in your community. Fill it with good simple food and a few extras such as a new dishcloth, a book of postage stamps, a bottle of hand lotion. As a family prepare and deliver your gift of love to a local center for the poor. In the evening, read together Matthew 25:31-45.

• Do something useless but fun today! Watch or read a version of Charles Dickens' *A Christmas Carol*, make gingerbread people, build a fire, listen to Handel's *Messiah*. Do something that enriches your soul and nourishes your spirit. Waste a little time with the Lord, who loves your play as well as your work.

• Send Christmas cards today to three people who wait for the mail to come to fill their day, for example, someone elderly or sick or far from loved ones. Be sure to include a little message of love with your name. Pray for these three this Advent day.

• Decorate your front door today. Let the world know that they are welcome in your house and that the birth of Christ is celebrated here. Saint Paul said, "Let hospitality be your special concern." As you put up your door symbol, meditate on ways your household might be more hospitable to neighbors, friends and family. What are the things that stop you from opening your heart and home to others?

• Share this day with a child. Take your young one to a Christmas place, perhaps a public crèche or a Christmas display. Help the child make or buy a gift for a loved one. Wrap this treasure and remind your child not to tell what's in it. Share a meal together or a special treat. End the time by sharing a book about Jesus' birth. (You might want to give the child the book as a memento of the day.) Listen well to your little one today; the Spirit often speaks through such innocence.

• Take a walk at night. Listen to the sounds of night. Allow the darkness to surround you. See the walk through the darkness as an opportunity to meet God. Think about Mary and Joseph and their walk into the darkness of unknown Bethlehem. What unknown "Bethlehems" do you face in the future? As you walk, turn these unknowns over to God, just as Mary and Joseph did. End your walk by joining the song of praise of God's night creatures—the crickets and owls, the traffic and the sirens. Hear their noises as a hymn to Emmanuel.

• Cook a casserole or basket of muffins for someone with too much to do and not enough time to do it. Drop it off with an offer to help in any way you can. It will feel so good to know that you cared enough to offer.

• Bring some living greenery (pine boughs or holly, a winter flower, a Christmas cactus) into your house today. Look at it, smell it, touch it! Remind yourself that our ancient Christian forebears saw the color green as a sign of God's unending love and hope. Let this greenery reign among your decorations as a sign of this marvelous Lover.

• Buy a Christmas candle today. Give it a prominent place in your home. Place your Bible next to it, opened to Luke's birth narrative. On Christmas Eve and every night of the Christmas octave (the week between Christmas and New Year's Day) light this sign of God's Son among us, read the word and delight in the wonder of it all.

• Make a simple Christmas decoration and place it next to your bed on a table or nightstand. Next to your decoration place a book that can prepare your spirit for Christmas. Every evening read at least one page from your book and enjoy your Christmas decoration as a reminder to savor simple pleasures in this very commercial season.

• Open the doors of your heart today. Give special attention, love and prayers to all those who come to the door of your home and workplace. Greet your telephone calls with the same hospitality and love. Welcome them all with generous attention; stop what you are doing and give them your full presence. Let this simple gift of self be a witness to the love of Christ among us. Your day will be more blessed and peaceful than you could ever imagine.

• Tell the people you live with—your children, your spouse, your parents—that you love them. Try to give each one a sincere compliment during the day. Pray that each member of your family may always know your love and the love of God. Remember that often your voice and your arms express God's love.

• Go Christmas shopping today. Don't go to the shopping mall. Go to some unique little shop. Maybe you can visit a favorite bookstore or neighborhood hardware store. Enjoy buying little, inexpensive things in this one spot. Be sure to wish the salesclerk a "Blessed Christmas."

• Put up your crèche today but do not put the Christ child in it yet. On Christmas Eve place the babe in the manger and read the story of Christ's birth to those with whom you share this holy night.

• Make or buy holiday breads today. Wrap them and deliver them to friends or neighbors. Before you deliver them, ask the Lord to bless these breads and bestow his deep and abiding presence on all those who share this bread.

• Ask forgiveness of someone you have hurt. Call or write, do whatever you must to make peace. If nothing comes to mind, ask the Lord to lead you to someone who needs your listening and understanding this Advent day.

Classroom Advent Activities

Adaptable for primary through junior high students.

• Read the story of the Annunciation (Luke 1:26-56) today. Act out the story as a play for another class. How do you think Mary felt when she said the words of the Magnificat? List words that describe how Mary might have felt after her visit from the angel.

• Wish your nose a Merry Christmas. Bring something to class tomorrow that has a "Christmas smell"—a piece of pine bough, a cinnamon stick, an orange peel, a candle—whatever smells like Christmas to you. Share your smells with one another and tell about a memory connected with this smell. Write a "Thank you for my Christmas nose" prayer.

• Write letters to people who have been important to you, who have helped you grow and learn. Thank them for all they have done for you. Share with them how important they are to you. End your letters with a prayer for their happiness and peace this Christmas. Send your letters to these special people as your Christmas surprise.

• Plan a Christmas cookie party. Have everyone bring four to six Christmas cookies to class tomorrow. Put all the cookies on a large platter and enjoy this treat at the end of the school day. After you have finished, give thanks to God for all the wonder and fun of these holy days.

• Listen to a Christmas carol today and learn all the words. Pick a carol that most people have never learned or the second and third verses of a popular Christmas song. When you go home tonight, sing it for your family.

• Get the name and address of a homebound person in your parish or community. Make a Christmas card for this person and write a cheerful note inside. Send a few each week until Christmas. Perhaps one or more people in your class can visit this person during the week between Christmas and New Year's Day.

• Write down the name of a person you know who could use God's loving help and your prayers. This person might be a sick relative, an overworked mom, a friend who has a problem, a famous person. Put all the papers in a basket. Pick one and tape it to the corner of your desk as a reminder to say a special prayer for this person each day until Christmas.

• This is "love your teacher" day. Do nice things for your teacher all day, but don't let on who is doing these things. Just do your good deeds because God loves this special person very much.

• Talk about the meaning of light in our Christian tradition today. Why do we put lights all over the Christmas tree? For homework tonight find out when and where the tradition of putting lights on Christmas trees began and why we do this.

• Do you have a good friend who lives far away? Today, write an essay about this person. Tell the class what makes this person such a special friend. Then write a short Christmas letter to this person and include a copy of your essay.

• Put the names of everyone in the class in a basket. Take a name from the basket. Be sure you don't get your own name. Do something nice for this person today, but keep it secret. When you discover that someone has done something nice for you today, believe that this good deed was a special touch of God's hand in your day.

• This is a day to fast. Decide on some way of fasting or doing without: not talking in the halls, not buying sugary treats in the cafeteria, giving up a recess to perform some useful task for the school. Whatever you decide, do it with a quiet love for the Lord who is coming so soon.

• Bring in some food goods for the poor today. Collect a box of nonperishable canned goods and boxed foods for the poor in your community. Be sure to include some fun items in your food box, such as jars of jelly and nice smelling soaps.

• Do something fun and useless today. Have an unscheduled art project, see a Christmas movie, work a crossword puzzle, have a Christmas spelling bee (using only seasonal words). Have fun together with no real purpose in mind.

• Create a Christmas card for your parent(s) today. Be sure to say "I love you" and offer your wishes for the best Christmas ever!

• Decorate your classroom door today. Draw outlines of your hands on green construction paper, cut them out and write your names on them with red crayon. With the fingers pointed down, build a tree-shaped pyramid of your green hands. On the very top, place a bright yellow star with the name of your class on it.

• Spend some time today with a younger brother or sister (if you don't have one, spend time with a friend's brother or sister). Read a story, play a game, go for a walk. For homework tonight, write about what you did with this younger person and how you feel about the time spent together.

• As a class, go to a darkened room. Sit together in the quiet dark space in absolute silence. Then light one bright candle. Watch how the candle fills the room with beautiful light. Listen to the carol "Silent Night." Really listen to the words as you watch the candle. Remember in your heart how the darkness felt and how the light felt. Remember that Jesus came to bring light to all of us and put away the darkness forever.

- For your homework today, write down a favorite Christmas recipe you always share at your house—a yule log cake, a Christmas salad, Aunt June's cookies, whatever. Share your recipe with the class and tell why it is so special. If you are really ambitious, put all your recipes together to create your own class Christmas cookbook as a surprise gift for parents this Christmas.

- For your homework today, bring to class some living plant that stays green all winter—a pine bough, a sprig of holly, an evergreen branch. Find out the difference between these specimens and plants that lose their leaves in winter. Notice the wonderful smells of these winter greens. How is God's love like these green plants?

- Christmas is a time for candles. The light of the Christmas candle reminds us that Jesus became the light of the world and still lights the way for all of us today. Find the paschal candle in your church today. Learn what the symbols on it mean, when and why we light the candle in our rituals. Ask your parents if you can have a special Christmas candle in the center of your table this Christmas.

- Bring old Christmas cards to school. Use them to design a small poster. Be sure to include a catchy slogan and lots of artwork. Use this poster to remind us that the real reason we celebrate Christmas is not because we get a lot of gifts, but because Jesus became one of us. Vote on the best poster. Take your creation home and put it next to your bed. When you awake in these days before Christmas, let your first thoughts of the day be about the coming of the Messiah and not about the things you might receive.

- Welcome everyone who comes through the doors of your life today. Let the people who walk into your school, classroom, home or bedroom and even the people who call you on the phone know that you are glad to be with them. Tell your Mom or Dad tonight how good it is to be home with them. Open the doors of your heart, school and home to everyone God sends.

- Jesus came into our world to teach us how to love one another. Tell two people you love that you love them. Try to find something complimentary to say to a friend today. Make sure it is an honest compliment, something you've been thinking but never took time to mention.

- Write an essay about being a giver instead of a getter. If you could give each person in your family one special gift of love, what would it be? Write about what would truly make the people in your family happy this Christmas.

- Find out how the nativity scene or "crèche" first came into use. Share with the class what your favorite nativity scene looks like. Do you have one at home? Have you ever visited a large, outdoor version? Why do you think people enjoy looking at these scenes?

- Are you holding a grudge against someone in your life? Is there someone you have never forgiven? Today, ask God to help you heal the wound in your heart that keeps you from forgiving that person. If you can, go to that person today and be reconciled. Start a new relationship. Forgive the way God forgives you.

Celebrating the Christmas Season

Hodie Christus natus est! Christ is born today! We do not know whether Jesus was born on the twenty-fifth of December, but historical data about Jesus are not nearly as important as the fact that we know, beyond proof and in faith, that Jesus the Christ took on human form, lived among us and calls us back to God as he invites us to live his gospel. This knowledge is what we celebrate at Christmas. Yet to celebrate on December 25 is no accident. The early Church chose to link the birth of Jesus with the pagan feast of the winter solstice. Early Christian thinkers infused new meaning into winter's darkness by declaring the darkest time of the year as the occasion of the birth of the new and eternal Light. Earth and heaven merge in a new reality.

With the first bells of midnight the fun begins. It is time to enjoy the preparations of heart and home with joy. Relax and enter into the wonder and fun of the day. Before you decide to do any of the activities suggested here, ask, "Does this activity enhance or hinder the Christ-life among us?" "Will the event bring us joy, or is it just one more thing to get done before Christmas?" Be selective about how you choose to celebrate. Give your schedule plenty of time for quiet. This is meant to be a season of joyful reflection. Allow for a generous amount of reflective time or all your busy ways will be wasted.

This day can be as joyous or horrendous as you allow it to be. Christmas turns into an overwhelming, exhausting experience in so many households because we overdo the celebration. We want to put every happy moment, every perfect gift, every loving moment into a day that just can't hold it all. In the process, we manage to crowd out the cause of the feast. I strongly recommend that you look at this day in a defensive way. Do battle against wanting too much, spending too much, even loving too much. Plan the feast well in advance. Leave ample time to relax and enjoy the company, the food, the gifts. Keep all these things simple.

We expect Christmas to be perfect, but in reality our homes are not like those in the magazines, we are not as handsome as the models in the commercials, and our tables don't look like the ones pictured in the gourmet cookbooks. Don't try to measure up to such standards. Keep Christmas in your hearts. Jesus wants to shine in a sanctuary of family love, not a picture-perfect scenario of a television holiday special. Be who you are on Christmas Day and enjoy the simple fun and profound meaning of the feast.

These suggestions offer a variety of ways to enter the feast of Christmas. Look at them with a sense of what fits your soul and how you can ritualize the journey to the manger. Let the rituals and symbols of Christmas be particular to your needs in the classroom and in the family.

Collecting Memories

As we look back on our own childhood Christmas memories, it is not the gifts received that we remember, but rather, the good times, the funny moments, the poignant events that stay with us. We retain little memory of how clean the house was or the menu of the day. What remains are the moments of love and joy: when Dad gave Mom his heartfelt gift and she cried; when Uncle Ed's chair broke in the middle of Christmas dinner; when little Billy sang a carol in the dark of his room when everyone thought he was sleeping. These moments become the treasures of Christmas past.

It is important for families to preserve and retell the memories of the past. As we revere our past we proclaim our history as the Church, the family, the people who are loved. We say to ourselves and to our children, "This is who we are. We are lovable and unique. We have been given great gifts." Christmas is a feast filled with such memory moments. As we nurture our children, it is important to share with them our family stories. The following are a few ways to preserve the memories of Christmas past.

An Ornament Collection

Each year make or buy an ornament for your child. Date the ornament and attach a small tag to it. On the tag, write something quotable the child said. For example, you might record what the child said when opening a favorite gift. This collection of ornaments plus any others they make or receive in the childhood years should be collected in a special storage box. You might want to add unique personal items to the hanging collection, such as a baby rattle, a favorite piece of jewelry or a small picture in a hanging frame. When the child leaves your household, you can present this box of memories with your best wishes as he or she begins a new phase of life.

The Family Ornament (F)

Each year make or buy a family ornament. Ornaments could be symbols of something important or memorable that happened since last Christmas—a vacation memento, a photograph of a loved one who achieved something special—or who died and achieved salvation! These small tokens will remind you of family stories. Be sure that every family member gets in the act of designing this ornament. Put aside some family time before Christmas to assemble your project. Make a tag for it with everyone's name and age and the date. Each year when you pull it from its storage box, you will remember the fun and joy that went into making it. Long after the days of family ornament projects, your tree will bring you the delight of little hands and helpful hearts that have grown up and gone on with their own Christmas.

The Class Ornament

Every teacher knows that each class is a unique blend of character and spirit. Suggest an activity before Christmas that lets students know how special they are. Design a class ornament that tells the story of who these children are as a class. Their symbol could tell about an event or honor they share, or it could commemorate an event that occurred in their school year. Just be sure it is like no other design. Put this new ornament on the class or school Christmas tree with those of past classes. Over the years through your teaching journey, the tree will chronicle for your students the history of your experiences as a teacher. Children will enjoy hearing about your other school Christmases. If you are in midstream in your teaching career, make some past-year ornaments from old photographs and gifts that you have collected. This is a perfect way to show off those handmade treasures that every teacher receives from generous hearts over the years.

Book/Video Collections

Both in the family and in the classroom, children's literature plays an important role in developing imagination, creativity and values. The great treasure of children's Christmas literature provides a wonderful source of inspiration as a child awaits the feast.

Each year acquire a book that tells the Christmas story in a new way. Two classics are O. Henry's story "Gift of the Magi" or Charles Dickens's *A Christmas Carol*. On the inside cover, write the date and the names and ages of the children who will share the book. Begin this collection and watch the delight in your children's eyes as these treasured books resurface to be enjoyed for another year. These books become the old friends of Christmas. Be sure to display your collection only between Christmas and New Year's and then pack them away till next year's visit. The book's inside cover is a great place to write your memories of each year's feast. The collection becomes a treasured display of memories as well as a valuable and fun resource.

A twist to this collection is to compile a video library of Christmas TV and cartoon specials and classic holiday films. You may want to restrict viewing time during the Christmas octave between Christmas and New Year by featuring a "special" film or cartoon each evening.

This is a delightful way to mark the family's growth. Your first books and cartoons will appeal to toddlers. As children mature the family Christmas library will include classics.

The classroom Christmas library takes on the added value of offering students an opportunity to integrate literature into the hectic, pre-Christmas curriculum. One story or chapter could be used each day as the thematic center of many subject areas: Discuss the book as part of religion class, plan a reading or grammar lesson using the book, give a writing assignment related to it or even incorporate it into a science, geography or history class.

You might want to let the students earn the funds to purchase their class Christmas book each year. Begin collecting nickels and dimes as soon as school begins so that your December purchase is well-funded. Inscribe all the students' names on the inside of the book. The book could be donated to a permanent collection in the school library as their Christmas gift to their school.

A Christmas Album

Photographs of special moments preserve stories of love and laughter and bring these moments to life again. These moments remembered and shared in pictures help build self-esteem. They say: This is my story. This is why I love and am loved. Christmas is a perfect time to celebrate love, to strengthen and uphold our family image and reaffirm our origins of love.

Start a Christmas album. Fill the pages with memories of past Christmases, pictures of each holiday year, favorite notes and cards. Every year add new pages. Write about how you spent the season, favorite gifts given and received, and touching moments. Place this album in a prominent place for everyone to enjoy. You will notice family members sneaking away with the album for a quiet reverie with their memories. The presence of this album and the reminders it offers can quell preseason stress as family members are reminded in pictures and words that their lives are rooted in love.

A videotaped record is another great technique to mark Christmas past. If you own a video camera, use it to record the lighting of the Advent wreath, putting up decorations, baking Christmas cookies, greetings from visiting loved ones, etc. Create a new tape for each year. You could include interviews with older members of your family asking them to share their fondest, funniest, even saddest Christmases.

In the classroom a Christmas album can reinforce the unique character of each class and be a real curiosity as students look back on their predecessors. Take a class photograph. Write about special school activities and projects in which the class participated. The fun of forming a special class identity in this album boosts the class's self-esteem and lets them know in a subtle way how lovable they are!

Another approach to this project is to make individual albums for the students. Let each student fill an album with pictures, Christmas essays, prayers, poetry and mementos. This holiday project is a perfect gift for parents.

A Collection of Toys

Toys are not just for the young. We all need to remember how to play. At Christmas, when we celebrate the birth and childhood of Jesus, we celebrate not only the children among us but also the child within us. Receiving and giving toys is a delightful way to do this. Start a collection of Christmas toys. Each year acquire one new toy that belongs to everyone who sits beneath your tree to play. You might add old and treasured toys to this collection. If you're creative, you might want to make some of the toys. Grandparents especially enjoy this activity. Notice how visitors react when they play with the toys beneath your tree. They will begin to arrive each year in joyful expectation of being able to play with your toys. When the Christmas season ends, put away your toys till next year.

In the classroom you might give students an opportunity to share some favorite playthings. Assign each child a separate day to bring a favorite toy to school. Allow time to share toys. Plan this activity before Christmas to help children assess what toys mean to them. Is it the latest fad toy that becomes their favorite? What is it that makes a toy enjoyable? Why do some toys lose their attraction soon after they are received? This exercise can balance the barrage of consumer advertising that overwhelms children in these pre-Christmas days.

A Tablecloth of Memories

Purchase a plain white tablecloth and a collection of permanent felt tip pens in a variety of colors. Put this tablecloth on your table each Christmas. You may want to put several layers of absorbent paper or heavy plastic beneath it. As guests arrive at your home during Christmas, invite them to autograph your tablecloth, write a special message or draw a Christmas doodle. As years pass and the tablecloth reappears on the Christmas table, it tells a story of how you celebrate Christmas in your home. Signatures of old friends and saints grace your table years after they first came into your Christmas.

Handmade Gifts and Cards

A handmade gift is a great treasure. The intangible qualities of another's work and love are priceless. Plan an activity for your family or class in which they make a gift for someone. Keep the project simple. Plan these projects well in advance of December and collect all the needed materials. Little ones could paint rocks that become paperweights for Grandpa and Grandma. Popsicle stick trivets are a favorite project for primary students. Older children can weave placemats, design coupons for chores and surprises such as back rubs, babysitting or cleaning the garage.

Set a date in early December for your gift-making day. If you're doing this as a family, be sure to involve everyone. Watch the delight and excitement as family members become engrossed in this activity. As the family or class works together, they learn a valuable lesson about Christmas: It is not what you give as much as how you give. After finishing projects, share a special holiday snack. Christmas cookies and eggnog, cocoa or hot cider serve as fitting reward for an evening of love and labor in the true spirit of Christmas giving.

Another possibility is to make your own Christmas cards. Create designs with stencils or stamps, or draw a design with black marker and reproduce it on a copier. In the classroom children can illustrate their Christmas cards and give them as gifts to Mom and Dad. Children's artwork never fails to express new insights into our more sophisticated images of the feast.

Christmas Card Writing Party
♡ 🍎

Invite friends and family together or spend a class period with the purpose of sending Christmas cards to anyone who is in need of your thoughts and presence this Christmas. Send cards to the poor and lonely, to politicians, to old friends and strangers. Let the card tell of your love for them this Christmas.

Crèche-making
♡

Saint Francis gave us the nativity scene. In Italian homes the family creates a crèche each Advent to display throughout the octave of Christmas. The crèche is burned at the end of the feast. This year, design your own crèche. Give each person modeling clay, white soap or soft wood and ask them to create one figure for the scene. Put it all together on Christmas Eve.

Sharing Christmas With Sister Bird and Brother Squirrel
♡ 🍎

It is a custom on many farms to leave a small portion of the crop unharvested as a gift to the creatures with whom we share the earth. In these barren winter days it is good for our souls to celebrate our kinship with all of creation by offering a Christmas treat to wild creatures.

Near the feast of Christmas leave a tray of seed, corn and nuts for the birds and animals that surround you. Offer this gift on Christmas morning and invite all the creatures of the land and air to join you in a hymn of praise to the newborn Messiah. As the birds come to share the feast, enjoy the first moments of your Christmas as moments of giving. Listen to the sounds of nature that welcome your gift.

In adapting this for the classroom collect enough pinecones for all students. Tie pieces of strong cord to the pinecones, then smear them with peanut butter and roll them in a bowl of birdseed. Let students hang their gooey gifts on trees on the school grounds.

These birdseed ornaments become a delicious treat for the local winged population.

As long as you are knee-deep in birdseed and peanut butter, you might want to let students make an extra pinecone treat to take home for their yards. This project also makes an excellent gift for someone who is homebound and can view the birdie treat from indoors.

A less messy activity is to put unsalted peanuts in the shell on your windowsill and watch Brother Squirrel enjoy a winter feast!

The Music of Christmas

Music often lifts us beyond the mundane into the realm of the spirit. Christmas carols not only remind us of the meaning of the feast, but the melodies fill our hearts with the memories, the feelings, the experience of Christmas. It is fitting to stop our busy preparations from time to time to savor the holy songs of the feast. These activities encourage hearing Christmas carols as prayer:

• Learn the story behind one of the traditional carols. Listen to all the verses of the carol as if you were praying the words.

• Attend a Christmas concert as a class or family. Make this event a special time together.

• Gather the family or class around your tape recorder or piano to sing Christmas songs with gusto. Invite others to your Christmas sing and enjoy the fun of remembering all the verses and harmonizing the easy parts! If you have a video camera, you might want to make a permanent record of the fun. Afterward, reward yourselves with some special holiday treats.

• Listen to a new Christmas recording. You can purchase one or borrow one from the public library or exchange music favorites with friends, neighbors, other teachers. Choose something you've never heard before. It is particularly enjoyable to gather in the dark and light the room with only the decorative lights of the tree and a Christmas candle. Ask everyone to get comfortable and sit in stillness for a short time. Begin the recording and savor the sound with reverence.

• Go caroling in your neighborhood and even turn your caroling journey into a progressive supper: At house #1, eat Christmas hors d'oeuvres. Carol to house #2, where you share a salad and to house #3 for a hearty soup or stew. Carol to house #4 where a well-deserved dessert awaits. If you have the appetite for this adventure but not the voice, you can bring along a portable cassette recorder as backup support for this night of music.

Another caroling option is to take your troupe to a nursing home or hospital. You can even carol for homebound or elderly parishioners.

The Feast of Lights

The use of light as a symbol of God's presence is most magnificent in the Christmas season. This holiday gives all of us an opportunity to understand the image of light as a wordless expression of God among us. Here are a few ideas that can encourage that understanding:

• Go for a ride on the nights before Christmas and visit the most notable light displays in your community. The dazzle and sparkle will awaken childlike wonder.

• Prepare a Christmas candle for your family or class. It can be simple or fancy. Place it next to the crèche. On the eve of Christmas or the last day of school, light your candle. Remind everyone that the candle is a sign of the presence of Jesus in your midst. Burn the candle throughout the Christmas season whenever you gather together.

• Plan a "tree picnic" for the day you put up your Christmas tree. Spread a tablecloth beneath the tree and serve a picnic meal of casual and simple food. Eat beneath the lights of your tree. Spend the mealtime talking about the meaning of the tree lights and remembering the significance and origin of your favorite ornaments. This picnic can end with the reading of a favorite Christmas story or poem. Let the night be devoid of television, radio and media noise. Entertain one another with your conversation and laughter.

Celebrating the Eve of Christmas

Christian families often have traditions for this night. Some serve special menus, some open one gift, some open all their gifts, some worship together on this holy night, some invite special guests. Whatever your customs, try to keep this night sacred, to reflect on the mystery of incarnation. You *can* celebrate a Christmas Eve that encourages this sense of the sacred in our midst.

• In many cultures Christmas Eve is a day for fasting. In Poland, for example, people abstain and fast till the first star appears in the night sky. As soon as children see the star, a great feast is spread on the table and the fast is broken to celebrate with joy the appearance of the savior's birth star. Begin a similar custom in your home. Spend the day fasting: Eat simple meals with no snacks in between. Watch for the first star of Christmas; when it appears, remove the Advent wreath, replace it with the Christmas candle and serve a feast of love.

• Hide the infant Jesus of your crèche scene. Ask children in your house to search for the hidden infant. Remind them that just as the Hebrews looked for the Messiah, so too must they search. Whoever finds the baby Jesus places him in the manger as the Christmas candle is lit.

• Plan a family prayer service for this night. Include the readings for the feast of Christmas. Ask everyone in the family to share a personal prayer at this time. End this prayer time with a period of silence so everyone can become aware of the presence of Christ in their midst. Close with a simple carol or hymn.

• Walk at night and watch Christmas unfold in the houses you pass. Listen to the sounds of the season of this joyful night. Be aware of the full spectrum of life around you. Pray for the people you pass. Praise the newborn Christ with the night creatures, the moon and stars. When you arrive home, share your reflections with one another. What homes seemed most joyful as you passed? What saddened you on this walk? When did you begin to feel the celebration of the feast? What gift did you receive on this night walk?

• Bake a birthday cake for Jesus. Prepare a Christmas cake fit for a king and plan to serve it as the evening wanes and bedtimes approach. Start a procession of children bringing the cake to the manger. Sing "Happy birthday, dear Jesus" and a variety of carols. Little ones delight in this ritual because in the cake and candles they really understand the reason for our happiness.

Beginning Christmas Day ❁

Begin Christmas Day with a simple family prayer of praise in the morning darkness. Then light the Christmas candle. You might want to give each family member a candle to light from this one candle. The family then processes to candles positioned throughout the house, lighting them and singing a carol or listening to Christmas music. The candles should be allowed to burn throughout Christmas day as a symbol that the Light is with us and we are filled with delight. (Caution is necessary! Children should not be left unattended with burning candles, nor should candles be left burning in empty rooms.)

Opening Family Gifts

Some families open gifts on Christmas Eve, some on Christmas Day. Some buy many gifts, some a few. Some wrap them, some simply place them beneath the tree. All this is a matter of style, tradition and preference. What remains as the important issue is that these gifts *never* replace the Lord as the cause for the feast.

Do whatever you must to keep gift-giving in proper perspective. Do not allow the consumer message that "things bring happiness" to influence the beautiful ritual of giving simply with love. As you purchase and make your offerings, keep in mind that these presents are meant to be symbols of your love for one another. They are meant to reinforce the generosity you feel for those you love. Set a limit to what you spend on these gifts and stick to it. Try to be mindful of family members with tighter budgets than yours. The gift says, "I am giving you my heart today." On Christmas the tokens of love we exchange should be shining symbols of the love that began in Jesus in the first birth cry.

A Few Guidelines for Christmas Giving

• Only one person at a time opens a gift while everyone else watches and enjoys the opening. After every person present has opened one gift, hold a short recess (perhaps ten minutes) while the receivers and givers can savor the gifts and the thoughts that went into the choices.

• Make as many gifts as possible. Handmade gifts are more valuable in the ways of the spirit than store-bought things. A hand-knit sweater, a Christmas poem, a painted rock paperweight, a woven potholder, a wooden toy—the list goes on and on. Start planning early and try to simplify what you give.

• Wrap your gifts in recycled paper, old Sunday comic paper, reusable bags. Be conscious of the need to conserve. Reuse Christmas wrap and trimmings whenever possible.

• Extended families who exchange names for gift-giving might try a yearly theme. For example, one year all the gifts could come from a yard sale or thrift store. The next year the theme could be crazy sweatshirts and T-shirts or perhaps subscriptions to obscure and interesting magazines. Another suggestion is to purchase tickets to an event that everyone attends together. This method of directing the gift-giving keeps things in proportion. It is hilarious fun to open the wild and strange things that result from this creative shopping invitation. It is important to exchange names very early. Whether you decide on a theme for giving or just use your imagination, this process takes some thought, time and effort, but it's well worth it.

• Give everyone at least one toy. Toys invite play. On this feast we need to relax with one another and play together. The child within needs to be honored on this day. Laughter, playful challenges and friendly competition allow the child in each of us to flourish. All too soon adults must return to their responsibilities. Let Christmas be a time of play.

Giving a Gift to Jesus

How strange it is that Jesus does not receive presents on Christmas! We open piles of Christmas bundles with little thought to giving a gift to Jesus. Little children love to prepare such a gift for the Lord. Ask everyone in the family to prepare a gift for Jesus. Young children can present him with a favorite toy; older children can offer the Lord a special pledge or project. These gifts for Jesus should be opened before any personal family gifts. Encourage the entire family to be serious about their Jesus gift. Put these offerings around the crèche scene throughout the Christmas season as a reminder of your intention.

The Feast of the Holy Family

The Feast of the Holy Family is ordinarily celebrated on the Sunday between Christmas and New Year's Day. We celebrate the reality that Jesus came from a family just like everyone else in humanity. His family name was full of history and importance. His ancestors were kings and beggars, prophets and fools. His family lived modestly and was not very upwardly mobile. His mother was pregnant before she married Joseph.

In this simple feast we also celebrate the wonder of family life. Family is the place where each of us—student, grandparent, mom, dad—is nurtured. Jesus' family life allowed him to grow into the vision the Father held up for him. The daily witness of Mary and Joseph in Jesus' early years helped Jesus to understand the power of love. It is no different for each of us. This is what we celebrate in this late December feast. The power of love given and received in the family becomes the Church's focus as we look to the life of Jesus and how his story becomes our own.

Family Night Party

Invite as many family members as possible. Serve foods that represent the ethnic background of the family. Ask each person present to share a memory of a family event that is either humorous or poignant or simply says this is who we are! If you can remember old stories that you heard from grandparents or others about the early days of your family, share them in addition to the more recent memories. Videotaping these wonderful stories would make the evening a permanent memory. This tape could be reproduced and given to new members of the family as a wedding gift.

Joseph Saturday

On this Saturday, get out the hammers, nails, drills and saws. Repair, sand, clean anything wooden in your house. Put the leg back on an old chair, repair the basement door, rehang the bookshelves. Do it all in honor of Joseph. Just as the original father-and-son team must have enjoyed their work together, your family can take this opportunity to work together. (This activity is also a great project for the feasts of Saint Joseph, March 19, and Saint Joseph the Worker, May 1.)

Family Album

Construct a family album. Let family members list the dates of their sacraments, important achievements, humorous anecdotes. Include important pictures and newspaper clippings. Try to go back as far as possible into the family tree. Each year on this feast of the Holy Family add the latest data to this treasured book.

Celebrating in the Classroom

Since schools are closed between Christmas and New Year's Day, these activities are perfect for return-to-school projects.

• Spend some time discussing Jesus' family tree. Discover why he was called the "Son of David." Do a family tree project with the class. Ask children to include the religion of each of their ancestors in addition to the usual information. Help children discover how the unique blend of heritage, religious and ethnic backgrounds makes them the special people they are.

• Read together some of the offerings of children's religious literature that discuss Jesus' family life. Ask children to write their own story about a day in the life of Jesus when he was their age.

• Ask children to bring in photos of favorite family members. Hang the pictures together in a prominent display area. Throughout the week, ask each child to tell a favorite story about the person in the picture.

Epiphany King Cake

You can enjoy the feast of the three kings by making a "King Cake." Bake a cake that includes a bean or small plastic infant Jesus (the size of a bean). The person who finds the bean or infant Jesus is treated like a king for the day and may choose activities and a television program to watch. In New Orleans "King Cakes" are served at parties until Mardi Gras. If you get the piece of cake with the infant in it, you must host the next party.

Gifts in the Epiphany Style

This method of receiving gifts was first practiced by a family who lived far from their extended family and would be alone in a new town for Christmas. It gives each day of the season a special meaning and creates an atmosphere of festival throughout the season. The Epiphany Christmas also teaches an important lesson in the process of giving and receiving rather than the content of the gifts.

In Matthew's Gospel we hear that the kings or wise men presented the Christ child with gold, frankincense and myrrh. On Christmas Day each family member receives three gifts. Then each day till the feast of the Epiphany the family gathers around the tree and opens one small gift: a box of crayons for a child, a bar of special soap for Mom, a special interest magazine for Dad and so on. These gifts can vary in cost and importance. On the feast of Epiphany everyone receives one last grand gift (something the receiver has been dreaming and wishing for). The evenings of Christmas become very exciting. This method of receiving creates a slower pace in which the gifts are savored and appreciated, in which there is time to affirm the giver of a gift. For young children this method eliminates the frenzy of opening a big pile of gifts and not really enjoying the objects received.

Celebrate 'Farewell Sunday'

On the Sunday after Epiphany invite friends and family to join you in the closing of the Christmas feast. Take down all the decorations, play the carols for the last time, eat the last of the cookies and cheese ball hunks! Pass a journal to the guests and invite them to record their best Christmas memory for this year. Share those memories over a simple meal of soup, salad and bread and say a final good-bye to this wonderful feast for another year.

Celebrating the New Year

New Year's Eve Talent Show

Invite friends and family to your home for an evening of untold talent. Each guest must prepare a performance for the rest to enjoy. No one is excluded from the requirement. What fun it is to watch Grandpa dance, Uncle Bob do magic tricks and Mom play the accordion! The last moments of the year fly by as the family enjoys the talent show and learns to appreciate one another in a new way.

New Year's Eve Family Film Night

Invite friends and family to share the year in film. Ask guests to bring this year's collection of family videos, slides and albums. Share summer vacations, birthdays and anniversaries in the closing hours of the year. This entertaining activity can be scheduled before or after a shared meal or even between the courses of a grand supper.

New Year's Campout

If you live in a temperate climate, this is a perfect occasion for a multifamily campout. If you are not the wilderness type, plan ahead to rent a big cabin in the woods, mountains, desert or beach. Joining family resources keeps the expense minimal, and the time together in this outdoor adventure creates memories for a lifetime. Ring in the new year around a campfire, sharing stories of years past, hopes for the future and joys of the present. Enjoy the company of good friends and simple pleasures.

This project takes planning, but the rewards are worth the efforts. Looking forward to an inexpensive time away as the holiday season closes banishes post-Christmas doldrums that come blowing in around the end of December.

New Year's Day ❤

The Christian tradition loves new beginnings! Christ offers each of us the hope of a fresh start as often as we can say *mea culpa* and pick up the pieces. New Year's Day is centered in the hope of fresh starts. Celebrate this day with a combination of quiet reflection and exciting promise.

This is a perfect occasion to attend a morning liturgy together as a family. Follow the liturgy with a family brunch. Serve a breakfast typical of a foreign cuisine. Each year surprise the house with another country's menu. It is interesting to see if the eaters can guess at what country's table they are feasting.

After the morning's activities offer family members an opportunity for quiet time: a walk in the neighborhood, watching a college football game on TV or whatever suits their mood. It might be a perfect time to recollect your thoughts about the coming year. What are your goals? What one new thing would you like to accomplish this year? What did you do last year that you would like to keep doing? Spend some time listening to the Lord's answers to such questions.

In the evening, gather around a table for which each family member has prepared one dish. Everyone must bring a contribution to the meal and must prepare it unaided. Don't bother coordinating this banquet. It's much more fun to allow creativity to take its course.

After supper, gather everyone for an evening time of prayer. This time should be centered on hopes for the coming year, a time of petitioning prayer. Ask everyone to prepare one petition prayer for each member of the family present. As you share these prayers of hope, light a candle for each person present as a sign of the life of Christ that promises to shine through the coming year in each family member.

Resolutions ❤

Making a promise to yourself to change your bad habits in the coming year is the classic invitation to failure. However, this proposition can be fun and rewarding if you invite those with you on New Year's Day to help you be accountable.

Ask all guests and family members to write down one small thing they would like to change in their lives in the next year. Then put these resolutions in sealed envelopes and place in a box to be stored with the Christmas decorations. The following year invite the guests to return to another New Year's Day supper. After supper, ask people to open their envelopes and share what they wrote and what happened. It is most gratifying and surprising to see the results! The simple exercise of making resolutions that you must be accountable for seems to give the effort an added dimension. In addition, this exercise points out how we change our expectations in a year's time, especially younger members of the family.

Burning the Cones

Here's a twist on the tradition of New Year's resolutions that you can do if you have a fireplace. In Sweden each member of the family is given a pinecone and asked to stand in front of a burning fire and proclaim a personal vice that the pinecone represents. Hold the cone high in the air, declare the "sin," then throw the pinecone into the fire. In this way you say good-bye to your fault and begin anew.

The Family Historian

On New Year's Day appoint one family member or a family team as this year's historian. The family historian collects memorable souvenirs and anecdotes of the family activities for the entire year. The historian's special talents—writing, art, photography and so on—contribute variety to the archives. On the following New Year's Day, the historian presents the family year for all to enjoy. The keepsakes, journals and mementos can be preserved in a box and dated for your family archives.

Back to School

On the night before school begins in the new year, give your child a final gift of the Christmas season. You can fill a supply box with fresh pencils, markers, erasers and crayons for the morning. For your teenagers, fill a box with an assignment book, new pens, comb and locker mirror. For college students returning to the dorm fill a box with personal care products and snacks. Starting back to school after the long Christmas break is more fun with a new collection of tools.

This is also a great time to give your child a winter book. On winter nights, this new book can fill that quiet time before bed or you can take some time out with your child and read this book together. Parents may want to tape a story or book so that young children in daycare can listen to Mom or Dad reading to them.

Junk Food Chart

The new year is notorious for diet resolutions. You can make a Junk Food/Health Food chart for each person in your family or class. High fat and sugary snacks are great once in a while, but often these treats are eaten instead of healthy choices. Keep a record of healthy foods eaten. For every three healthy choices, the person can choose one junk food item. This simple method of making food choices teaches us to respect and care for our bodies as the loving Creator intended. 1 Corinthians 10:31 speaks about using what we eat for the glory of God. This Scripture could be placed on the chart as a gentle reminder to make wise choices.

The Babysitter Box ⬓

The days of January and February can be dull and dreary. Parents can use a break from children to enliven their marriage. Children may not look forward to being "stuck" with the babysitter while Mom and Dad are having fun. To alleviate this problem, create a Babysitter Box. Simply fill a storage box with toys and activities that can only be enjoyed when the babysitter is with the children. The sitter is delighted with this box full of fun, and children look forward to opening the Babysitter Box each time Mom and Dad leave them.

Adopt a Family for the New Year ⬓

You don't have to look far to find a needy family who could use your help. In January contact your church and ask for the name of a family struggling with a personal burden, perhaps illness or unemployment. Each month do something special for this family. You can deliver a meal, buy tickets for a sporting event or movie, do something that will bring a little sunshine into their lives.

Celebrating Valentine's Day (February 14)

This is a day to celebrate love. There are many opinions concerning the origins of this day. Some say it was a Roman fertility feast; some believe it was linked to Saint Valentine, according to tradition an early Roman martyr; some trace its beginnings to the old English belief that the birds choose their mates on this day. Whatever the source of this celebration, it offers us a chance to brighten the winter with words of love. The following suggestions offer new ways to say "I love you."

Lover of the Year Award ⬓ 🍎

As a class or family, nominate one person who showed unselfish love in the last year. Send this person a handmade certificate that expresses the honor "Lover of the Year"; express your admiration and tell the award winner why he or she was chosen.

**Secret
Valentine Pal**

Choose a name of a family member or class member and prepare a surprise treat for that person on this day. This could be a box of candy, a flower, a new book with a little note that says, "From your secret pal with love!"

**Valentine
Poem**

Write a poem each year to someone you love. Even if you are not a poet, the creative juices might be sparked by your love. Mothers and fathers can write little poetic gems to their children. Children can write poems to their grandparents.

In the classroom announce a Love Poem Contest. Recruit a judge from outside the class or school and announce the winners on this day. Display the entries in the hall or publish the winners in the church bulletin or school newsletter.

**Making
Valentines**

What an expense store-bought cards can be! Why not make your own? Gather a collection of paper, doilies, stickers, glue, markers and crayons. Then plan an evening or weekend before Valentine's Day to create your own cards. These handmade love notes will mean so much more to the receiver than the commercial version.

Think about sending valentine cards instead of Christmas cards. In the dreary days of February a surprise love note may be much more appreciated than another "Season's Greetings" card in December.

**Valentine's
Day Vacation**

Use this winter feast to get away from the ordinary. Surprise your spouse with a night at a hotel. Enjoy an evening of quiet intimacy. In the morning ask the babysitter to bring the children for brunch and a swim in the hotel pool. This winter vacation splash may be just what you need to lift your spirits.

**Hidden
Valentines**

Instead of handing your valentines to each other, hide them throughout the house. Little ones love to find hidden treasures. Looking for love messages is a great activity for housebound toddlers. To keep children guessing, give clues to the whereabouts of the special treasures.

**Valentine
Placemats**

Make a valentine placemat for the members of your family or class. Arrange the cards each has received on a piece of lightweight poster board. Then ask family members or classmates to write qualities that make the person so lovable, such as, "likes to laugh" or "always thinks of others." Cover the placemat with clear plastic contact paper.

Valentine
Breakfast
♡ Serve a pink breakfast to begin love day with a bang! Add red food coloring to pancake batter and milk. If you are a creative cook, make heart-shaped pancakes with a cookie cutter.

Valentine
School Lunch
♡ Pack a brown bag decorated with heart stickers. Inside the bag put a love note and a special treat such as a red balloon or a red rubber ball.

Heart's Desire
Dinner
♡ Plan a valentine supper made up of every family member's favorite. You can then serve the crazy combination with a sense of humor. Chocolate ice cream and lima beans or pizza and broccoli make for great fun on this day of love.

Celebrating Other Winter Feasts

Hanukkah
(December)
♡ The Jewish festival of lights is celebrated about the same time as the Christian Christmas. Check a calendar for the date each year. Research this feast or invite a Jewish friend or relative to your classroom or home to explain its rituals. Be sure to find out about Judah Maccabee. Create your own menorah, a special candleholder with eight candles, one for each night of Hanukkah. Light one candle each night of the eight-day feast.

December 2
Isaiah
♡🍎 This is a day to celebrate Isaiah the prophet. Isaiah and John the Baptist are the great saints of Advent. Read Isaiah 43: "I have called you by name. You are mine says the Lord. You are precious to me!" Make a list of the names God calls you. Then list the good names you hear about others you live and work with or go to school with. Tell one of them a name they may not have heard.

December 6
Saint Nicholas
♡🍎 In Holland and other European countries, this feast is celebrated by putting out a stocking or wooden shoe on the night of December fifth. The saint visits in the night and leaves treats of nuts and fruit.

This is a great time to communicate with the saint of generous love. On the night before the feast, put out a stocking or shoe and include a letter to Saint Nick. Ask children to talk to the saint about what they hope for during the feast of Christmas. The next morning the children will find goodies in the stocking and a return letter from the saint (thanks to a parental secretary!). This letter tells the child of God's great love for us and the true meaning of Christmas. It might also offer a few suggestions on how the little ones might become more saintly themselves before Christmas!

Another fun idea is to deliver secret stocking surprises to older folks, college folks and even "Scrooge" folks on the sixth of December. Prepare some Christmas stockings with treats, address them and leave them in creative places: Aunt Pearl's mailbox, your college son's dorm room, the boss' desk top. Just like Saint Nick, do this generous deed anonymously!

December 8
The Immaculate Conception

This is Magnify the Lord Day. Join Mary in magnifying God's presence in the world today. Go to the grocery store, the shopping mall, the subway station—any scene of short tempers and hectic life. Stand in the midst of the place and offer a silent prayer of praise to God. You might recite the Gloria or your favorite praise prayer to yourself. Let the secret power of praise fill the earth.

December 10
Thomas Merton

Thomas Merton died on this day in 1968. Merton was a Trappist monk and spiritual leader. Celebrate his life by seeking some silent place to meet God on this day. As a group or individually, light a candle and sit with God without saying a word. "Be still and know that I am God" (Psalm 46). Feel the presence of God within.

December 12
Our Lady of Guadalupe

This is a day to celebrate Our Lady with Catholics of Mexican heritage. In 1531, the virgin appeared as a young, pregnant Aztec maiden. Begin the day with the "Hail Mary." If possible recite this prayer in Spanish. Offer a toast to Our Mother with hot chocolate and sweet treats. For the real adventurous, serve *menudo*, a hot tripe soup. At this time, the gardens of western Mexico produce the first fruits of winter's bounty. With your tripe soup serve a large "Guadalupe" salad filled with Mexican delights in honor of the virgin who brought forth roses in December.

Menudo (Tripe and Hominy Soup)

Menudo is a soup of tripe and corn or hominy. It is a classic part of Christmas holiday meals in Mexico. A bowl of *menudo* is said to cure a hangover and to have other medicinal powers.

    5 pounds tripe*
    1/2 pound veal, cut in small pieces
    1 tablespoon cooking oil
    3 cloves garlic
    1 tablespoon salt
    1-1/2 cups chopped onion
    1 teaspoon chopped cilantro
    2 tablespoons chili powder
    8 cups water
    1 large can hominy
    2 tablespoons lemon juice
    chopped green onions and cilantro or fresh mint

*2 pounds precooked pork may be substituted for the tripe. While this is not authentic *menudo*, it is more palatable for the faint of heart!

Cut tripe in 3-inch pieces. Brown the veal in 1 tablespoon of oil in a large kettle. Add tripe, garlic, salt, onion, cilantro, chili powder and water. Cover and simmer for eight hours until the tripe is tender. Be sure to add more liquid when necessary. Add the hominy and heat, then add lemon juice. Serve with a garnish of green onions and cilantro or mint.

Bunuelos (Fried Sweet Puffs)

This is a favorite Mexican pastry served on Christmas Eve and other special occasions.

    3-1/2 cups all-purpose flour
    1 teaspoon salt
    1 teaspoon baking powder
    2 tablespoons sugar
    1/4 cup butter or margarine
    2 eggs
    1/2 cup milk

oil for deep frying
confectioners' sugar

Sift flour with salt, baking powder and sugar into a bowl. Add butter with a pastry blender until it resembles coarse meal. Beat eggs and milk together and stir into dry ingredients until a ball of dough forms. Turn ball out onto a floured surface and knead for 3 minutes or until the dough is very smooth. Cut dough into grape-size pieces and let rest for 20 minutes. Roll each ball out on a flour board so that it is about 4 inches in diameter, and cut a hole in the center with a thimble. Fry in hot oil (375 degrees) until puffed and golden, about 20 seconds on each side. Drain on a paper towel and sprinkle with confectioners' sugar.

December 13
**Saint Lucy's
Day**

In Sweden on the feast of this saint of light the eldest daughter rises early and prepares fresh pastries for the household. She carries the breakfast to her parents' bed with a wreath of lighted candles in her hair. Share in this tradition with a breakfast of warm coffee cake or rolls and coffee or tea in honor of Saint Lucy. Place a lighted candle on the breakfast table.

Saint Lucy's name is derived form the Latin word "lux" or light. In the old Julian calendar (before our current Gregorian calendar) December 12 was the longest night of the year. On Saint Lucy's Day we celebrate that the inner light of Christ outshines the darkness. This is a wonderful time to record the length of daylight and give thanks for the coming of the Light.

Go out into the night and look for Saint Lucy stars, the early morning/late night meteors that flash across the December skies.

December 16
Las Posadas

Tonight the Advent novena *Las Posadas* starts. The custom brings neighbors together as they leave their homes and go house to house asking for lodging in memory of Mary and Joseph in Bethlehem. This is a day to reflect on the ways of hospitality. Invite to your classroom or home someone who immigrated to this country. Ask them to share with you their experience of welcome or unwelcome here. Resolve to see strangers as wayfarers who, like the Virgin, are bearers of Jesus. This is a wonderful time to do something for the homeless. Take a field trip to a homeless shelter and work in the kitchen. Collect soap and shampoo for a drop-in center. Send a cash donation to a center for the homeless.

December 17
The 'O's'
🏠🍎

Today we begin the "O" antiphons for the final days of Advent. From December 17 through December 23 we listen to the titles of Jesus that have become familiar to us through "O Come, O Come Emmanuel," the ancient Advent hymn of praise.

> December 17: "O come, O wisdom from on high"
> December 18: "O come, O come, O Lord of might"
> December 19: "O come, O flower of Jesse's stem"
> December 20: "O come, O key of David, come"
> December 21: "O come, O daystar shining bright"
> December 22: "O come, desire of the nations"
> December 23: "O come, O come Emmanuel"

To celebrate the "O's" create symbols for each of the antiphons. Make simple ornaments with these symbols to use as tree decorations. A lamp for wisdom, a rock for might, a rose for Jesse, a key for David, a star for the daystar, a globe for the nations, a baby for Emmanuel.

At home, this activity could be turned into "O" cookies. Bake sugar cookies in the shape of these symbols. Decorate your tree with them or give them to all who enter your house during the holy days ahead.

December 26
Kwanzaa
🏠🍎

Kwanzaa is an African-American family observance that begins on this day in recognition of the African harvest festivals. *Kwanzaa* means "first fruit" in Swahili. Kwanzaa is a celebration of family and values that begins on December 26 and continues till January 1. The seven principles, or *Nguzo Saba*, are featured during the week, one each day. The seven principles are: unity, self-determination, collective work, cooperative economics, purpose, creativity and faith. Each day of Kwanzaa a red, green or black candle is lit and the family reflects on the principle of the day. Cultural and historical gifts are exchanged to enhance the meaning of the day's principle. These universal values align well with the values of Catholic education.

In the classroom several students could explore the history of Kwanzaa and its originator, Dr. Maulana Karenga. A resource for this project is *The Story of Kwanzaa* by Safisha L. Madhubuti (Chicago: Third World Press, 1989).

December 27
The Festival of Tachiu
♡

The festival of Tachiu is a Taoist celebration in Hong Kong. It is a day set aside for peace and renewal. Enjoy a little renewal in this busy month. Plan to set aside time this day for a quiet walk, a good book or a long nap.

December 29
The Battle of Wounded Knee
♡ 🍎

On this date in 1890, two hundred Native Americans died at Wounded Knee Creek, South Dakota. Sioux women, children and men died as the U.S. Army conquered and slaughtered them. The Dakota land was taken from the Sioux in this bloody battle. In the spirit of these Native American martyrs, pray for an end to the bigotry and greed that remain in our country today.

January 5
Saint John Neumann
🍎

This saint, who lived from 1811 to 1860, rode his horse, Geraldine, through the wilderness of America to celebrate Mass for the people of his large diocese. He was the first American bishop and author of the first American catechism. These books taught pioneer children about our Catholic faith. On this bishop's feast, ask students to write a letter of thanks to the bishop of your diocese. Introduce yourselves to the bishop and offer him your prayers.

January 15
Birthday of Martin Luther King, Jr.

Martin Luther King, Jr., is the prophet of equality and civil rights in our day. His life stands as an example for all of us to seek justice for those who have suffered from bigotry. During the week of his birthday, celebrate his courageous life in thought-provoking ways.

🍎

'He Had a Dream...Do You?' Essay Contest

Have a school-wide essay contest. Using Martin Luther King, Jr.'s dream for a more just world as a focus, ask students to write essays about their own dreams for justice. Announce the winners of the essay contest on King's birthday. Prizes for the winners could be a copy of King's "I Have a Dream" speech or a picture of Martin Luther King, Jr.

🍎

Peace March

Organize a simple march for freedom on this day. Ask each class to design a peace banner to carry in your nonviolence march. If possible, march through your school neighborhood in quiet reverence. When you return to the school say this prayer:

God, today we remember Martin.
He lived and died for the virtue of justice.
He yearned for the day when all your children
would be treated the same.
Help us to see one another with your eyes,
eyes that love equally.
Help us to care with your heart, a heart that makes no
separation or distinction.
Help us to bring the peace and justice
that Martin dreamed about
to our little portion of your kingdom. Amen.

The Prejudice Hour

On Martin Luther King, Jr.'s birthday, play this awareness game: Announce to your class or family that all brown-eyed (or another characteristic such as curly hair) people have superior qualities. The brown-eyed people are smarter, richer, better looking and so on. The blue- and green-eyed people are less acceptable and not as smart, rich, capable, etc., as the wonderful brown-eyed people. Spend one hour deliberately favoring the brown-eyed people. At the end of this time, ask the blue- and green-eyed people how it felt to be treated in this manner. Ask brown-eyed people how they felt.

January 17
Saint Anthony of the Desert

This saint is the patron of domestic animals. Saint Anthony spent many solitary years in the deserts of Egypt. Perhaps he befriended animals to keep him company. To commemorate his day, create a collage of cat and dog pictures to hang in the classroom. Ask students to write a poem that describes their favorite pets. At home have a party for your pet in honor of Saint Anthony. Serve hot dogs or hush puppies for dinner. You may want to serve only vegetarian dishes on this feast of a great animal lover! Rent a classic movie about a famous animal, for example, *Lassie Comes Home* or *National Velvet*.

January 20 **'Ask Not What Your Country Can Do for You'**	On this day in 1961 President John F. Kennedy made his famous inaugural speech in which he said, "Ask not what your country can do for you. Ask what you can do for your country." Make a poster illustrating the kind of things students can do to make the United States a better place to live. Pray today for the needs of our country.

January 24
Saint Francis de Sales

Saint Francis de Sales said, "You can catch more flies with a spoonful of honey than with a hundred barrels of vinegar." This is a day to say kind things to those you meet and to keep a smile on your face. Ask your students to smile at three strangers today and to offer three honest compliments to family and friends. Then, ask the students to keep a journal of the reactions to their "honey." Share the results the next day in religion class.

African-American History Month
(February)

During this month celebrate African-Americans who have contributed to the wealth of our American life. Here are a few important dates.

February 1 — Birthday of poet Langston Hughes
February 4 — Birthday of Rosa Parks
February 5 — Louis Lautier admitted to National Press Club, Birthday of baseball player Hank Aaron
February 7 — Birthday of composer Eubie Blake
February 9 — Birthday of author Alice Walker
February 11 — Harriet Tubman Day
February 12 — NAACP founded
February 16 — Birthday of actor LeVar Burton
February 17 — Birthday of singer Marian Anderson
February 19 — Birthday of jazz singer Nancy Wilson
February 20 — Frederick Douglass Day
February 21 — Malcolm X assassinated
February 23 — Birthday of educator W.E.B. Dubois
February 25 — Hiram Rhodes Revels became a senator
February 27 — Birthday of journalist Charlayne Hunter-Gault

For an excellent African-American awareness project in the classroom, ask students to choose one of the people on this list and create a poster, mobile or poem about the life of this person. Each day of the month one figure could be presented.

February 2
**Feast of the
Presentation**
🍎

This is the day we commemorate Jesus' presentation at the Temple in Jerusalem. Luke's Gospel (2:22-38) tells us that Simeon recognized Jesus as a light to the nations. We, too, are called to be light and salt for the world. Celebrate this simple prayer service based on Matthew 5:13:

Materials needed: a Bible, a bowl of unsalted peanuts, a bowl of salted peanuts, a packet of salted peanuts for each person.

Gather students in a circle. Ask each student to take an unsalted peanut and eat it. Then read Matthew 5:13. Pass the bowl of salted peanuts and ask students to eat one of these.

Discuss the following questions:

Describe the difference in the two kinds of peanuts.
Which did you like best? Why?
How does the salt make the peanut taste better?
Why does Jesus want us to be like salt? What does that mean?

Give each child a packet of peanuts to take home. Close with this prayer.

Lord, help us to be salt that flavors our world.
May we bring your joy to this school,
your love to our families,
your care to the old and lonely.
May our friends want what we have,
because they see the flavor in our lives that comes from you.
Amen.

February 2
**Candlemas
Day**
🏠

The Feast of the Presentation is also called Candlemas Day. It is a traditional day to bless the candles we use in church. Blessed candles are used in our homes as quiet lights of prayer. In the midst of storms, illness and special needs Catholics traditionally light blessed candles to symbolize their prayer for God's care. Remember this day by purchasing a sturdy three-inch candle to use as a "family victory candle." Every time a family member experiences a victory, light this candle for the evening meal. Light your family candle in celebration when someone gets a good grade on a difficult test, makes the basketball team, gets a promotion, recovers from an illness and so on.

February 2
Groundhog
Day

Groundhog Day traditionally is the first announcement of the hope of spring. If the groundhog sees his shadow, spring is on the way. Make shadow puppets to celebrate this day. Shine a light behind your hands and move your hands and fingers to make shadow animals on the wall.

During school recess, play a game of shadow tag in honor of the groundhog. The person who is "it" tries to use his or her shadow to tag another person's shadow.

February 3
Saint Blaise

This bishop of Sebaste in Armenia is the patron of sore throats. In many churches, a special blessing of throats is imparted on this day. The power of prayer and faith in healing the body is an important part of our faith tradition. Invite someone who has experienced the Sacrament of the Anointing of the Sick to your class to tell about the experience.

February 22
Moses

This Old Testament "saint" deserves a feast day. Read about Moses' life in a children's Bible. Then make a burning bush to decorate your class or dining room table.

Paint a twiggy branch with red paint and anchor it in a solid base of styrofoam. Tear up small pieces of red, yellow and orange tissue paper. Crumple the paper and glue it to your bush. Add tissue randomly till the bush is a blaze of color. Make a small sign to place at the base of the bush that reads: "I Am Who Am!"

February 22
George
Washington's
Birthday
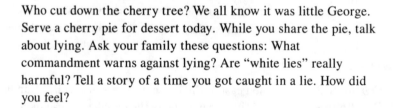

Who cut down the cherry tree? We all know it was little George. Serve a cherry pie for dessert today. While you share the pie, talk about lying. Ask your family these questions: What commandment warns against lying? Are "white lies" really harmful? Tell a story of a time you got caught in a lie. How did you feel?

February 29
Leap Year
Day

When you are given this extra day, plan something unique that you will remember for years. Do something you've never done before—eat a foreign dish, visit a new place, learn a new skill.

In the classroom you can make a Leap Year time box. Fill a shoe box with things that describe life at the school, church, community. Include the price of a loaf of bread, your favorite movie and song and whatever you want to remember about this time. Keep the box until the next Leap Year Day, when you can open it and see how much has changed.

The
SPIRITUALITY

of
SPRING

In our Christian tradition, Lent is a time to get rid of our junk, a kind of spiritual, psychological and physical housecleaning. As spring looms on the horizon, everyone is energized by a shift in the weather to longer, warmer days. This energy forces us to abandon our tired winter ways to make room for new life. The season frames the Church's journey through Lent to Easter well and serves to call each of us into the mystery of transformation in Christ.

The word *Lent* comes from the Anglo-Saxon word meaning "spring" or "longer days." This liturgical season began in the early fourth century as a time when those who were preparing for baptism on Holy Saturday entered into a period of fasting and intense prayer. As the practice continued the spirit of this spring prayer journey was extended to the whole faith community as a preparation for Easter.

Family life moves with the seasons, too. Children are bored with winter activities. Parents are equally bored with such comments as, "I have nothing to do" and "Mom, make him stop looking at me!"—all of which stem from having nothing better on their minds than stirring up a little negative excitement. Winter confinement forces the whole family to be a little too familiar with our own good and bad habits. The family, as the domestic version of the Church, faces Lent as a time to open the windows of our hearts, minds and bodies to the potential for new beginnings, a time of rebirthing grace. This dynamic offers a new energy, a grace, that can make these forty days not a begrudging "giving up" period, but a season of rejuvenating our tired spirits.

In the classroom life can become mundane as schedules develop into patterns. Even dynamic teachers are challenged to keep learning exciting when students become bored with these patterns. Lent and the whispers of spring invite us to think in new ways and open mental and spiritual windows for a little of the Holy Spirit's fresh air. Lent challenges us to change and grow into more than we thought we could be. The tempo of life begins to speed up as both student and teacher stretch their souls toward new potentials.

Families and classrooms can jog their Lenten spirits into the mood of the season by simple signs and practices. These activities provide tangible expressions that keep our Lenten efforts in perspective. They encourage creativity in emptying ourselves for God.

Celebrating Lent

Ash Wednesday

The season of Lent starts on Ash Wednesday. This day marks the fortieth weekday before Easter Sunday. The day takes its name from the custom of Christians marking their foreheads with ashes in the form of a cross. This striking symbol is a visible sign of the beginning of an inward change of heart. Take your family to the Ash Wednesday liturgy and wear the ancient ashen cross. On this first day of the forty, let your outward pride fade into the humility of wearing the cross of those who seek forgiveness.

Making a Real Easter Basket

On Ash Wednesday, place a shallow tray filled with potting soil in a plastic-lined basket. Plant grass seed in the basket. Put this basket on the dinner table or classroom windowsill. Throughout Lent watch the grass begin to grow and reflect together on the journey from death to new life. Watch the barren soil spring to life in a lush green carpet. This real Easter basket can be the centerpiece of the Easter table.

Little Blooms to Easter

A flower chart helps young children mark Lenten days. As each day of Lent passes, or with each good deed or experience, they can add a paper flower or a flower sticker and watch their Lent bloom. Use a large calendar or make a chart for the six weeks of Lent.

Family Meal Time

Make family meals a special concern during Lent. Lenten meals need not be occasions for austerity. Families can use this time to learn to eat more wisely and simply. Mealtime provides an opportune time for family members to share the happenings of the day in quiet leisure with one another. Our shared experience is another form of nourishment, feeding our hearts and spirits.

Look at the amount of time you spend at the table. Does this time compete with television or other activities? Do you tend to use this time as a forum for correction or criticism? If quality mealtimes are a problem for you, begin this Lent by designating one day a week to gather the whole family for dinner. Serve a simple meal everyone enjoys. Then take the time to listen and interact with one another in an affirming and caring way.

Begin this family meal with a shared prayer. Each week of Lent a different family member could be in charge of the prayer before the meal. Encourage younger children to add to these prayers by asking questions such as: "What good thing happened to you this week that you would like to thank God for?" or "What smells so good on our table? Would you like to thank God for that smell?"

Lenten Prayer Corner

Make a family prayer corner somewhere in the house. Find a quiet spot for peace and recollection. Perhaps you can put a comfortable chair near a sunny window with a small table next to it. Place the Scriptures and Lenten readings there. Put a small crucifix on the table. Encourage family members to spend a little time there each day. Don't forget to enjoy the luxury of this place yourself.

The classroom, too, should have a permanent prayer corner that children use throughout the year. During Lent, extend this corner by creating a place where students can quietly read spiritual books and the Bible. Each day, display the daily readings from the liturgy or a short verse from Scripture in this corner. Put a crucifix on the wall in this area and place a small Easter basket beneath the cross with a pencil and paper next to it. Invite students to write special prayer requests and place them in the basket. At the end of each week, pray together using the papers in the basket.

Displaying the Cross

Make a simple cross from two branches or hang a store-bought cross on a prominent wall in your home or classroom. Add the inscription: "If you love me, take up your cross and follow me."

If you have an outdoor area for display, make a large cross to erect in the schoolyard during Holy Week. This cross can be used in an outdoor Way of the Cross service.

Wearing the Cross

For centuries Christians have worn simple crosses to remind them of their discipleship. Use this time to encourage your family or students to wear a cross or crucifix (a crucifix is a cross with the figure of Christ on it). Simple wooden crosses can be purchased inexpensively. You might like to distribute these to your family or students when you make commitments to perform Lenten resolutions. The cross reminds us gently to keep the disciplines of the season.

The Poor Box

Establish a poor box for the season. Every time you save money by buying lesser cuts of meat, eating a meatless meal, eating at home rather than at a restaurant, choosing not to rent a video or see a movie, walking instead of driving—whatever you can do to save a little bit—put the savings in your box. On Good Friday empty the box and donate the money to your favorite charity.

Examine Your Conscience Together

Forgive someone against whom you hold a grudge, and encourage your children to do the same. Hold a simple evening prayer time to call to mind the need to forgive in our lives. Share ways in which you would like forgiveness in your household. If you have noticed some hurtful or unloving actions during the week, bring them up at this time. Close the prayer time by reading Colossians 3:12-13.

The Rock

The entrance to the tomb of Jesus was closed with a huge rock. This rock was so large that when the women came to the tomb they thought they would need help moving it. We all have hard places in our hearts and lives that keep us from meeting the Savior. These rocks prevent us from loving one another. To develop this idea, put a large rock and a permanent felt pen in the center of the table or in your prayer corner. Encourage family members or students to write on the rock the things that keep them away from growing in their relationship with Jesus. Young children might write "fighting with my brother" or "not doing my homework," while teenagers might sneak up to the rock to write "worrying too much about grades." Moms and dads might write about spending more time listening to their children. Let the rock fill up with this reconciling graffiti during Lent and watch the hard places in your hearts disappear.

The Sacrament of Reconciliation

Prepare your family to participate in your parish reconciliation service. Support your parish community in this liturgical event. Your participation speaks loud and clear to your children of your belief in the sacramental life of our Church.

In the classroom spend extra time reviewing the importance of the Sacrament of Reconciliation. Design invitations for students' families from the Good Shepherd, who personally invites them to the parish reconciliation service.

Proclaim a Fast

Fast and abstain from more than food this Lent. Discuss with the family some common bad habits. Look at what positive steps you can take together to change unhealthy ways. Resolve to listen more attentively to your spouse, work as a family at picking up messy rooms, attempt to limit the house noise of radios, phones and television. Resolve to cut down on the amount of driving and use of gasoline.

This attempt at fasting is not for God's benefit. We need it to put our family life in a more loving perspective. It is not so much that we deny ourselves as it is an attempt to seek a more life-giving way to live in God's presence.

Paschal Candle

Make your own paschal candle. Decorate a large candle with Easter symbols as well as your family name. Light this candle on Holy Saturday night and pray by its light.

For a Lenten art project, students can design their own candles for use with their families, adding personal symbols that represent their faith and the joy of Easter. Paper cutouts can be glued to the wax, melted crayons can be used for paint, and colored tissue paper can be decoupaged in place with white glue.

Cocoon Project

This is a great opportunity to do a little collaborative learning. Purchase a cocoon kit from a science catalogue or local natural science store. Arrange to begin this project about two weeks before Holy Week. It takes just a few weeks for the butterflies to emerge from their cocoons. As children watch the cocoon become a butterfly share the story of Christ's death and resurrection. Out of the darkness of death comes the hope of new life. For younger students share a children's story based on this theme. A good choice is the book *Hope for the Flowers* by Trina Paulus (Mahwah, N.J.: Paulist Press, 1972).

The Purple Paper Chain

This project came from a grade school in New Orleans, Louisiana. Students there created a chain of purple paper that extended completely around the interior walls of the school hallways. Each week the students added links for each act of love they performed in the previous school week. By the end of Lent the school was literally surrounded by love. This could be a wonderful family project as well. The purple chains could encompass the interior walls of the kitchen or family room.

'Me-less' Day

Invite family members or students to spend a whole day not using the pronoun "me" or "I." Give each person five safety pins. Tell them to make chains of the pins and attach them to their shirts. If you hear another person using "me" or "I," you can ask for a pin. The person with the most pins at the end of the day receives a reward. This simple game calls attention to how much time you focus on yourself. Adolescents especially find "Me-less" Day painful yet enlightening.

Temple Field Trip

Our Christian heritage finds its roots in the Jewish faith. Lent is a perfect time to plan a trip to a local synagogue or temple. You might even plan an exchange program between young students of the temple and those of your church. To understand the Jewish faith gives rich insight into the life of Jesus. Be sure students understand that the Jewish people weren't responsible for the death of Jesus. With older students you might want to discuss the abuses that resulted from such erroneous assumptions in the past. As you prepare to celebrate Holy Thursday look at Jesus' spirituality in light of his Hebrew roots. You might consider celebrating a Seder meal in your home.

Sponsor a Third World Child

Decide as a class or a family to sponsor a child through a Christian mission agency. This project witnesses to the beatitudes in a direct way; it also teaches the joy of helping those in need. Display your child's picture and pray for your child daily. Encourage family members and students to contribute from their own savings to support this distant sister or brother. This project can continue long after the Easter lilies have faded. Keep your Lenten hearts throughout the year as you reach out to the Third World poor.

Beatitudes Bulletin Board

This project is useful on a classroom or kitchen wall. Create a bulletin board or poster that features one beatitude each week of Lent (see Matthew 5:3-11 for a list of the beatitudes). Ask students to find pictures or news articles that feature each week's beatitude (e.g., "Blessed are those who mourn"). At the end of each day pray for the people added to the display. This simple project brings the awareness of human suffering into focus and offers a view of the world that keeps the message of the gospel alive in our daily lives.

John 12:24 Project

All of us need to understand what it means to "die to self." This project brings the meaning home and helps gardeners get ready for their spring planting. Prepare planting trays with potting soil. Put flower or vegetable seeds in a small basket next to the soil. Make a sign with the quote, "I tell you the truth, unless a kernel of wheat falls to the ground and dies, it remains only a single seed. But if it dies, it produces many seeds" (John 12:24).

Every time family members or students do a selfless act of kindness, they can plant a seed. The new seedlings can be transplanted into the garden during the Easter season as living reminders of Jesus' words. Use seeds that are easy to grow (marigold, impatiens, etc.) and adapt well to transplanting.

Celebrating Holy Week

Holy Week is a time when all the symbols, the drama and energy of our faith come together for one dynamic, faith-filled experience. The liturgies of this week express the very identity of our discipleship. In our families and classrooms we should revel in the gospel stories of Jesus' passion, death and resurrection—for in these stories we find the seeds of faith. Children and adults need to smell the chrism oil, break the bread, watch the vigil fire and play in the waters of baptism. It is a week to touch the symbols and soak up the wonder of the paschal mystery. The following activities encourage the child in all of us to live the drama of Holy Week.

Monday of Holy Week

This is the day to make your plans for the week. Plan to attend your parish liturgies as a family. Get babysitters for your preschoolers, plan easy meals so that you are ready to get out the door in time for the evening services. The effort will seem too great without a little preplanning. Let your family know ahead of time the "what and when" of these family times.

The Easter Tree

Spray paint a small twiggy branch white. Then ask your young children to make caterpillars by rolling pipe cleaners around pencils. Hang the caterpillars on the tree. On Holy Saturday remove the caterpillars and replace them with butterflies made from wallpaper scraps, bright-colored magazine pictures or construction paper and crayons. Add bits of colored tissue paper as flowers. The butterflies remind us of our new life in Jesus. On Easter you can add colored eggs and other symbols to your tree.

New Clothes

It is a tradition in many families to wear new clothing on Easter as a symbol of our new life through the Resurrection. An "Easter outfit" should mean more than being the best dressed in the Easter parade! Plan ahead and purchase one new item for each member of your family. Whether it's a new tie for dad or a hat for little daughter, let everyone "put on Christ" in new garments.

Tuesday of Holy Week

Make a Holy Week Garden

Find a small garden spot outside and plant some spring flowers. Then create a small tomb out of modeling clay and set a big rock next to the tomb. On Friday add three small wooden crosses. On Saturday put the rock in front of the tomb. On Easter morning roll away the rock, remove the crosses and put a piece of white cloth in the tomb. Read the appropriate sections of the passion story as you make these changes in your Holy Week garden.

The Rock

Write on your rock (see page 72) all through Holy Week. On Easter remove the rock and read the story of Easter morning when the rock was removed from the entrance of the tomb. Replace the rock with an Easter candle.

The Secret Basket

Purchase an empty Easter basket and fill the bottom with plastic grass (or shredded paper from the office). Ask everyone to add items to the basket throughout the week. On Easter Sunday deliver the basket to someone who is lonely and needs this joyful treat.

This gift basket is a great outreach project for the classroom. Ask each student to bring in one item for the basket. On the last day of school, ask a volunteer parent to deliver the basket to a homebound parishioner. If possible, take this person's photograph with the basket. Share the photo with the class upon their return to school.

Great Wednesday

Chrism Oils

This is the day the holy oils are distributed to churches for use in the rites throughout the liturgical year. If possible, attend the Chrism Mass celebrated in your diocese. The diocesan newspaper or parish bulletin will have the date, time and place for this liturgy at which the oils are blessed.

At your evening meal on this night, bless a small bottle of oil. You might want to use bath oil or essential oil from a specialty store that sells crafts supplies, candles and potpourri. Use this oil at home in the coming year. The ancient custom of using oil for comfort, healing and anointing can become a new and meaningful tradition in the domestic church, our homes. On this night after the oil is blessed, ask everyone to anoint each others' forehead with oil in the sign of the cross.

**Holy
Thursday**

Make Bread

Invite the whole family (or class) to make bread from scratch today. If this isn't possible, buy frozen dough, let it rise and bake it. Serve the bread whole and let each person break a piece from the loaf.

The Maundy Meal

This is a family meal full of symbols. Prepare a centerpiece of grapes and bread for the Eucharist, a coin purse for Judas and a lantern for the soldiers in the Garden of Olives. Serve thirteen things to represent the number of guests at the Last Supper. Conclude the meal by reading John 18:1-9.

**Good
Friday**

Proclaim a Fast

On this solemn day agree as a family to spend the entire day talking quietly to one another and fasting from noise. Turn off radios and TVs and unplug telephones and stereos. Live this day in quiet reflection with God. Pray and fast as a family. Rest in the presence of the Lord and hear the voice of the Spirit among yourselves.

Color Red Eggs

Dye some eggs red to recall the legend of the first Easter eggs. The legend tells us that Mary Magdalene went to Pontius Pilate on Easter morning to tell him of the Resurrection. She brought him a gift of eggs. Pilate refused the gift and said he would not believe Jesus had risen unless the eggs turned red. In an instant the eggs turned red and Pilate believed! Eat these eggs on the night of the Easter Vigil.

Preparing Easter Eggs

This is the night to create eggs for the feast. The egg is a symbol of hope in new life and has been a part of Easter menus since A.D.

700. Here are some ways to get creative with your eggs:

• Use plastic eggs to hold little symbols of the feast: a rock (for the tomb), a piece of white cloth (for the shroud), a cross (for Jesus' death). Let children collect the symbols and tell their meaning. Reward anyone who knows all the meanings.

• Put Easter promises in real eggs. Pierce the ends of raw eggs and blow out the yolks. Color the eggs. Then write down things you will do with your child: a walk, a trip to the zoo, lunch with grandpa, cleaning grandma's house, making cookies for a neighbor, etc. Roll up the slips of paper and push them inside the eggs. In the classroom, have children make a promise egg for their parents. Crack the eggs on Easter to discover the promises of love. These eggs can be used to decorate an Easter tree. Plastic eggs can also be used.

Holy Saturday

Making Breads

On this "tomb day" make your Easter breads. You might want to make hot cross buns, sweet yeast rolls decorated with an icing cross. These breads are symbolic of Christ's rising and victory over the cross.

Easter Baskets

Fill baskets with alternatives to sugary sweets. Try fruit, cheese and surprises from the grocery shelves that are usually too expensive for everyday cupboards. Everyone in the house should receive a basket. Fill Dad's with a jar of smoked almonds and some gourmet steak sauce, Mom's with a jar of apricot preserves and a box of herbal teas. Teenagers love kosher dill pickles and mozzarella cheese sticks. See the grocery aisles as a treasury of Easter surprises for everyone. Top off the basket with a few nonedibles such as pencils, crossword puzzle books, puzzles, games, hair ribbons, etc.

Make a Lamb Cake

Use a mold to make a cake in the shape of a lamb. This traditional Easter dessert represents the paschal lamb who was slain.

Pray for the Catechumens

Assign each member of your family or class one of the new

members of your parish who will be received into the Church this night. Pray and fast for these people all day. Send them notes today expressing your joy over their decision to be a part of your Church. In your note, share with the new member why you like being Catholic and what it means to you to be Catholic.

Trimming Trees and Planting Gardens

Some Eastern Rite families traditionally plant their spring gardens on Holy Saturday. This is a good time to trim back the dead wood that has accumulated over the past year. In the evening this wood can be used to build an outdoor Easter fire in celebration of this holy night. If it is too early to plant the spring garden, you might use this day to plan your garden and order seeds from seed catalogs. Let every family member grow a favorite flower or vegetable or try a new exotic vegetable.

Celebrating the Easter Season

The celebration of Christ's Resurrection is not a one-day event for the Church. We savor the feast for fifty days, until the feast of Pentecost. Keep this in mind as you plan your spring. Each day of the Easter season can offer some reminder of resurrection. The prayers of our Easter liturgies focus on the great privilege we bear as believers in the Resurrection. Keep the joy of Easter morning in your spirits throughout the season. Do everything you can to promote the Alleluia feeling at home, in church and in the classroom. Easter is not just a holiday full of bunnies and eggs; it is an attitude of inner joy that stays with us long after the jelly beans are gone.

Visit Some New Life!

Use spring vacation to visit newborn animals. Go to the nearest zoo, petting farm or pet store and enjoy the babies. This experience brings us back to the simple wonder of creation.

Star of the Week

Each week of the Easter season designate one member of the family to be "star of the week." The "star" gets to ride in the front seat of the car with the driver, choose favorite television programs each evening and choose the menu for Sunday's supper. You can plan other privileges that fit into your family life: favorite cookies, favorite board game, inviting a friend over to spend the night. The idea of this week is to affirm the unique and special people in your family as a sign of God's love for each of us.

Godparents' Supper

One of the most inspiring parts of the Holy Saturday liturgy is the baptism of the catechumens. This moving ceremony reminds all of us of our own baptism as we join in repeating our baptismal promises. This season is a great time to host a supper for your godparents and the godparents of your children. If the godparents live far away, send them an Easter card or make a phone call to let them know they are in your thoughts.

The Emmaus Walk

In the quiet of the second Sunday of the Easter season, take a solitary walk. If there is a picturesque spot near your home, go there to enjoy the beauty around you. As you walk imagine that Jesus comes to walk with you. Talk to him about your deepest needs as you walk. Then, listen to the thoughts that come to mind as if Jesus is responding to your words. You might try the Emmaus walk as a group venture. Ask everyone to take a solitary walk, then return to the group and share what happened.

Respect Life Baby Shower

During this season, contact a local center that supports the life of the unborn or a day-care center for children of high school mothers. Ask for a list of gifts needed for these babies. Host a baby shower for the center in your home or classroom. Serve snacks and play games if you wish. You might invite a local representative of the pro-life movement to share ideas with you.

Celebrating Mary

M ary is honored during the month of May as the unique and privileged soul who was chosen to be the mother of God. Mary is seen as the advocate who brings the needs of all humanity to the heart of her son, Jesus. Here are some new ideas to celebrate Mary, based on the traditions of our Church.

Mary Day

Designate one day in early May as Mary Day in your church and school. Plan a full day of activities honoring her. Some parishes begin with a liturgy focusing on the Mother of God. The rosary is prayed in the afternoon. The day could conclude with Evening

Prayer and a potluck supper. Invite a speaker or view a video on the Church's Marian teachings. Whatever you do, make this a day of prayer and learning about Mary's place in our faith.

Circle of Roses
⬡ 🍎

The word *rosary* means a circle of roses. It was intended to convey that each Hail Mary is like a rose and our prayers form a circle of prayers that we offer to heaven. Mary is often pictured with roses at her feet. The use of the rosary developed in the Middle Ages as a substitute for the Liturgy of the Hours for those who could not read. The 150 Hail Marys represented the 150 psalms, and the mysteries of the rosary became simple signposts for the events of the Gospels.

Today, the rosary is a popular devotion. This beautiful ritualized prayer and the use of rosary beads as a method of meditation have an honored place in our tradition. The month of May is a perfect time to introduce this devotion to children. If your children do not have a rosary, it is a great project to make one from a kit available at a religious supply store. Then explain the prayers to them. Pray the rosary at least once during May as a family or as a class. It will leave a lasting memory with everyone.

Wearing the Blue
⬡ 🍎

The color blue is traditionally associated with Mary. Pick a special day in May to wear something blue in memory of the Mother of God. Another way to remind ourselves of our kinship with Mary is to wear a small, blue ribbon the entire month. This ribbon can be threaded with a small religious "Mary" medal or other symbol of the Virgin. These blue ribbons make perfect remembrances of the parish's Mary event. Young children love to wear these bows with the tiny medal attached. The little symbol makes honoring Mary very real to primary grade students.

Signing the Magnificat
🍎

The Magnificat is Mary's hymn of gratitude and praise (Luke 1:46-55). Mary's absolute trust in God is displayed in her beautiful canticle. To enjoy the power of the Magnificat learn to sign the prayer using the international symbols for sign language (find a book at the public library or invite a signing person to teach you). To further highlight the meaning of the prayer, sing it with the signs. This project is a creative communion meditation for school liturgies, as well as a lesson in the art of signing.

**Outdoor
Rosary With
Mini-plays**
♥ 🍎

You can turn the rosary into a dramatic event by taking the beads outdoors. This exercise can be done as a block rosary or as a school project. Assign each class or family a specific mystery of the rosary. Ask them to create a still scene of living statues to depict the Gospel event. Give each class or family a location along the prayer route for their scene. In a neighborhood, each family could use their front yard for their scene. At school, each class could be assigned a different spot on the church grounds. At home, the family could create small scenes with statues on shelves in various rooms.

The entire group begins together. As you reach the first mystery, those who are in the scene leave the group and portray the mystery. The entire decade is prayed in front of the scene after the mystery is announced. You can add a short meditation before the decade if you wish.

This walking journey of prayer is an active way to pray the rosary, especially for children. This outdoor version is a good way to keep them involved and reverent when more stationary versions cause distractions. Another approach is listening to an audiocassette version of the rosary. This devotion is perfect for long car rides or even with earphones as you walk for exercise.

**Origami
Bouquets**
♥ 🍎

Origami is the Japanese art of paper folding. This ancient art form is simple, yet produces beautiful results. During the month of May, make paper origami flowers for Mary's bouquet. The public library offers ample resources for origami. You can use lightweight paper to make roses, lilies and a variety of flowers that last forever.

In the school each class can learn to fold a different flower. These paper bouquets can be displayed at the foot of Mary's statue during the month of May. This art project is a way to unite art instruction with the liturgical signs of Easter and Marian devotion.

Celebrating Mother's Day

This commercial occasion to give Mom a card and a gift can become much more than a money-spending event. People feel guilty if they ignore Mom on this day, yet they feel manipulated into buying the cards, perfume and flowers pushed on this day. Here are some noncommercial giving ideas that say "I love you" without a price tag.

Memory Box

Every Mom receives loads of loving mementos from her children throughout the parenting years: love poems, painted rocks, "I'm sorry" notes and so on. Make a box in which she can keep these memories. A sturdy cardboard box with a cover will do nicely. Decorate the box with self-adhesive paper, paint, pretty wallpaper or fabric. Label the box with the words, "Mom's Memory Box."

The Twenty Questions Tape

If you would like a gift that Mom will treasure for years to come, make an audio or video cassette gift. Record children answering questions about their mothers. Young children love to describe their moms on these tapes. Ask the child: "How tall is your Mom?" "What is Mom's favorite color?" "What does Mom do at work?" These kinds of questions often result in delightful responses.

Recipe Book

Ask all the moms of your students to submit a recipe that is her child's favorite. Let the students recopy these recipes with their own reflections on why this selection is their favorite and any special memories of when it was served. Ask each child to include a drawn or written portrait of their mom on the recipe page. Assemble all these gourmet treats in one volume. Make copies of your cookbook and let the students give them to their moms as Mother's Day gifts.

Create a "Mother's Cookbook" for your family. Ask all members of your extended family to submit a favorite recipe that their mother or grandmother created or made often. Compile all the entries in a binder and present this family collection to all the households. Save a few copies as gifts for future brides who will join the family ranks.

New Mother's Album

Do you know a young mother who is celebrating Mother's Day for the first time? Give her a little collected wisdom for her mothering career. Ask all the mothers and grandmothers who know her to respond to the question, "What is the best advice you would offer to a new mother?" Include their responses in their own handwriting, or write or type them yourself. Put all the responses in an album. Present the album and a small bouquet to the recipient. The album will prove a treasure of wisdom and insight that will encourage your new mom for years to come.

Mom-of-the-Year Award

Ask your family or class to reflect on someone they know who has been a great mom in the last year. Perhaps the choice will be a mom who is a dedicated school volunteer, a mom who has stood by the bedside of a sick child, a mom who drives the soccer team to its games, a mom who cares for her own parents. Send that mom a special card that expresses your admiration for her virtue. Let her know that she is a living witness to the love of God. Each year pick a new "Mom of the Year" and enjoy the fun of surprising someone else's mom.

The Story of Our Mothers

If you have a daughter who is grown or almost grown, you will enjoy creating this legacy for her to treasure. Collect a picture of each of her female ancestors (Mother, Grandmother, Great-Grandmother, and so on). Next to each picture write the words, "This is _____, the mother of _____, the mother of _____" in the style of the Old Testament patriarchs. Write a little story about each woman. Tell about her life and times; tell about her struggles, her goodness, her faith. Tell any anecdotes that have been passed down through the ages. If you cannot find a picture of these feminine ancestors, simply use a drawing of a woman of that period. Your daughter will form strong connections with her heritage through this collection.

This can be a great creative writing, history and religion project for junior and senior high school students. It can be given to a mother from her son or daughter.

Coupons for Mom

Ask children to design coupons and write on them the tasks or household chores they can perform: "Clean the kitchen for a week"; "iron ten articles"; "a back rub"; "a week of packed gourmet lunches"; "water the plants for one month." Redeemable whenever she wishes, these coupons will mean more to Mom than any purchased gift.

Queen for a Day
♡

Moms don't get a day off very often. Let the whole family get into the act of doing everything Mom usually does: Cook meals, straighten the house, etc. Let Mom pick the entertainment for this Sunday or weekend. She can decide to take a family walk, see a movie or stay home and watch her favorite video. To start this day off on the right note, give her a card or banner before she gets out of bed. Present her with the official declaration that she is Queen for a Day. Bring her breakfast in bed, the Sunday paper and a bouquet of spring flowers. Let the whole day ring with your love for her.

Celebrating Other Spring Feasts

March 1
Go Fly a Kite
♡ 🍎

This windy month is a perfect time to fly a kite. You can invite children and their parents to a kite-flying contest. Ask each child-parent group to design and build a kite. The first Saturday in March gather everyone at an open field to see whose creation can fly the longest and highest. Be sure to award the winners. Follow this fun with a brown bag lunch.

March 6
Michelangelo's Birthday
♡ 🍎

This Renaissance artist left a legacy of wonderful paintings, sculptures and architecture. To celebrate his genius, hold a birthday party for him. Decorate with pictures of his paintings and buildings. Serve Italian cookies. Ask each person to mention a favorite Michelangelo work of art and why it's a favorite. Get out a history of art book and play a game of Renaissance art trivia.

March 8
Saint John of God
♡ 🍎

This saint founded a religious order dedicated to caring for the sick. To celebrate the feast, invite a health-care professional to the classroom and let students interview this person. Ask the person to share with the class the ways in which this work is ministry.

Take time out to write to your favorite nurses, doctors, nursing home workers or parishioners who visit the sick. Tell them how much they are appreciated. Thank them for their generous spirits. Pray and fast for these dedicated ministers on this day.

March 16
Saint Sarah

Sarah, the wife of Abraham, became a mother in her old age and is the grandmother of Judaism, Islam and Christianity. The story of Sarah teaches us that nothing is impossible with God. Sarah's great charism was that she had enough faith to "go with the flow."

On Sarah's feast spend time with your grandmother. Visit her, write her a letter, visit her grave. In the home or in the classroom, share stories from your grandmothers' lives that enriched your own faith. Invite a grandmother to share her life story with you on this day if your own grandmother cannot be with you.

March 17
Saint Patrick's Day

Pot of Gold

Hide a little "pot of gold" in lunch bags on this Irish feast. Put chocolate gold coins in a napkin in the bag along with a green cookie. Be sure to include a little "blarney" on a note.

A Patrick Fire

Legend tells us Patrick introduced the Easter fire to the Church. Fire symbolizes the fire of God's love and Christ as our Light. On this night build a fire in your fireplace or go to a park and build an outdoor fire. As you watch the flames share the story of Saint Patrick and invite everyone to join you at the Easter Vigil service as the Church proclaims, "Christ our Light."

March 19
Saint Joseph

Celebrate Joseph as the father of Jesus. In Italy this day is the occasion for extravagant meals. A plate is set at the table for Saint Joseph and it is filled with food. After the meal, the extras are taken to the hungry and poor. This practice of giving food to the poor in honor of Joseph could become a canned food project. On March 19 ask everyone in your school to bring canned foods to the statue of Saint Joseph or a large container labeled the "Joseph Pot." Take this offering to a local food pantry.

As a family, prepare a meal for someone who is sick or unemployed. Deliver it with a "Happy Saint Joseph Day" card and your best wishes and prayers.

In the school celebrate the feast of Saint Joseph with a special morning liturgy. Invite all the fathers of the school and parish. After the liturgy, invite the dads to the classrooms for a breakfast of juice and donuts. When students return home that evening, remind them to honor Dad with a special treat or act of kindness.

March 20
The First Day
of Spring
⬟🍎

Celebrate the spring equinox by putting fresh flowers in your house or classroom. Put a pot of fragrant hyacinth on the bedside table of a nursing home resident. Put a sweetheart rose on a friend's desk with a note that says, "Happy Spring." Arrange a vase of daisies on the kitchen table. Start a compost pile for future flowers. Let the blooms proclaim that spring has sprung!

Use the first day of spring as an excuse to go for a walk. Americans typically spend over ninety percent of their time indoors. Walk around the block, listen to the sounds of life around you, stare at the trees, the sky, the water, the sand. When you return, read Psalm 104.

⬟🍎

For the Birds

Another first-day-of-spring project is to build a home for the birds. You can purchase a kit in a nature store or craft shop. Hang it in a quiet spot and watch some parents-to-be set up spring housekeeping in your creation.

⬟🍎

The First Bloom

Don't forget to set your house in order with spring's arrival. Clean the yard in preparation for earth's greening. Offer to prepare the yard and home of an elderly person for spring. Wash windows and shake the dust out of winter carpets.

If you live in a climate where winter is frosty and spring brings new flowers, hold a contest to locate the first spring flower. When the first daffodil or tulip emerges, plan an outdoor supper for that day. Roll out the grill and cook some picnic favorites. Eat the meal outdoors if possible or take your summer fare inside as you celebrate the wonder of new life.

⬟🍎

Spring Garden Contest

Have small groups (classes or families) design a spring and summer garden for the neighborhood community, church grounds, hospital grounds or other public area. Each group must plant and maintain their garden plot. Award a prize for the best effort.

March 22
Gutenberg
Bible
🍎

This is the day the first printed Bible appeared. To celebrate this historic event ask students to bring their family Bible to class. Ask everyone to pick a favorite verse from the Bible and memorize it. Have a Bible Bee: Read the first part of familiar lines from Scripture. Ask contestants to complete the line or phrase. The last one standing wins.

March 25
Annunciation
of Mary
🏠🍎

This is "Hail Mary" day. Pray the words of this ancient prayer with a reflective pause after each line. Gather your family or class together and say this prayer with new meaning on the day Mary agreed to become the Mother of God.

🍎

A Yes Note

This is the day Mary said yes to God. How are you asked to say yes to God? Write the word *YES* on one side of a piece of paper. On the other side, write some ways you are called to live out this yes. Ask Mary's help with your yes. Carry this note in your pocket all day.

🍎

Yes Button

In the classroom make YES buttons in honor of Mary, who said yes when asked to become the Mother of God. Ask students to wear the buttons all day. Encourage them to share the meaning of their buttons with anyone who asks. The next day, have students share the moments when they were asked what the button meant.

🍎

Music Appreciation—Ave Maria Style

Listen to Shubert's or Gounod's beautiful musical version of the *Ave Maria*. Listen to the music with a sense of prayerfulness. This occasion presents an excellent opportunity to explain the Latin words to our children. This ancient language is part of our Catholic heritage, yet the post-Vatican II generation has little understanding of its meaning. Learn another beautiful Mary hymn found in your church's hymnal.

April 1
April Fools'
Day

This is a day for silliness and having fun. Taking time to play is important to our well-being.

Brown Bag Silliness

For lunch, ask students to pack a lunch that they are willing to trade. Be sure parents know about this ahead of time. Each lunch should contain a sandwich, a piece of fruit and a snack. In addition, everyone should include a note with a riddle on it. Put all the lunches in a pile and have students choose one different from the one they brought. After lunch, ask others your riddle until someone offers the correct answer. Remember to thank your donors for the delicious April Fools' Lunches.

Silly Supper

Let everyone prepare one part of the meal. Each contribution to the supper must be a secret, silly surprise. For instance, serve a pitcher of blue lemonade (add food coloring); "smiling applesauce" (make a smiling face with raisins for each serving); Dr. Seuss' "green eggs and ham"; gummie worms in chocolate pudding for dessert. Many such "silly recipes" can be found in children's cookbooks.

April 5
Saint Noah

Noah is the Old Testament hero of the Flood and the patron saint of sailors and boat builders. On his feast day, build a miniature raft from craft sticks or twigs. Give your "ark" a name that reminds us of one of the virtues Noah needed to survive the flood (e.g., "Hope"). Float your creation in a nearby stream, pond or ocean, or in a birdbath, pool or even a bathtub. If more than one person makes a raft, have a race.

April 10
Arbor Day

In many states Arbor Day is celebrated on this date. *Arbor* is the botanical name for "tree." Support the ecological system by planting a tree. These valuable resources return oxygen to our atmosphere. Plant a tree at home, in a local park or at school in memory of a loved one who has died. This reminder of someone for whom you grieve stands as a living symbol that life does not end with death. Free trees are often available from government agencies, local forestry offices, etc. If you can find a resource for free trees, let each child plant a tree. In the classroom you might invite a forester to speak to students about the value of trees or discuss the value of the rain forest to our earth.

Yom Hashoa

On this Jewish feast, all humanity recalls the agony of the Holocaust. The date varies according to the Jewish calendar; it corresponds to April 10, 1945, the beginning of the Allied liberation of Auschwitz. To honor those who died during the Holocaust have a three-minute period of silence at noon. Share the story of Anne Frank with your family or class, or perhaps another story of the Holocaust.

April 23
The Feast of Saint George

This saint protected the Crusaders in their return to England. He is known as the slayer of dragons. We all have dragons in our lives, those ugly things that need to be done that we ignore. The more we ignore our dragons the bigger they get! What are some of the dragons in your life? Cleaning the attic, calling Grandma, balancing the checkbook? On this feast of the Dragon Slayer, make a list of three of your biggest dragons. Slay these three monsters today and be on the lookout for future dragons.

Shavuot

Shavuot (Shah-voo'-oat) is a Jewish feast celebrated seven weeks after Passover. The date varies, so check your calendar. It is a harvest festival. Families ate a hearty meal of the spring crops and grains, and always left some grain in the field for the poor. This is a thanksgiving meal in gratitude to God for our rich blessings. In the tradition of Shavuot, prepare a basket of fresh breads or muffins and take it to a local soup kitchen along with a cash donation.

May 1
May Day

This ancient festival of spring is celebrated with dancing, songs and games. It was originally celebrated to insure fertility and new life. The maypole dance symbolized the never ending circle of life and reproduction. In ancient communities children were given little baskets filled with treats as gifts of gratitude for their presence.

We can enjoy this May feast by doing a little dancing ourselves. Roll up the rug and have a May square dance. Borrow a recording from the library or get together with other families and hire a caller. Spend a spring evening learning this fun country-western dance.

In school May Day dancing could be a great physical education activity. Instead of the regular curriculum, each class could learn a different ethnic dance—learn to clog, learn an Irish jig or the tango. At the end of the day, gather the whole school and have the classes perform their new dances for the assembly. As an alternative you might want to invite a group of ethnic dancers to share their gift with you.

May 5
Tango No Sekko

The Japanese Feast of Kites is still celebrated in Japan. Kites were first used in Japan as communication tools in warfare in the thirteenth century. Now, kite-making is a beautiful art in the Japanese culture. Silk and paper kites sculpted into intriguing shapes dot the skies of Japan on this day.

Take time out to play on this day. Make or purchase a type of kite that you have never flown before. Take the kite to the beach, desert or field and watch it soar in the wind. After the fun, enjoy a Japanese meal or just an old-fashioned American picnic.

Memorial Day

Memorial Day began as a day to honor the nation's war dead. Now this holiday, celebrated on the fourth Monday of May, has expanded to include all those who rest in our cemeteries. Make a visit to an old cemetery today. Enjoy the beauty of the plants and trees. Take some typing paper and #2 pencils and do a collage of gravestone rubbings. Put an American flag on a forgotten soldier's grave and stand in silent prayer for this hero. Read Thornton Wilder's play *Our Town* and meditate on the precious gift of life that we celebrate on this day of memories and honor.

Memorial Stones

Create a small centerpiece at home or in the classroom. Collect an assortment of small stones and arrange them in a shallow tray. Put a small American flag in the center. Ask students or family members to write on the stones the names of people they know who have given their lives in service to their country. Encourage viewers of your centerpiece to pick up the stones and pray for the person whose name they hold in their hands.

Visit With a Veteran

In class before Memorial Day have students invite relatives who served in America's wars to visit your class. Ask them to share their experiences and bring any medals, uniforms, mementos or pictures they may have. This visit brings history right into our midst and is a lasting lesson.

Peacemaking on Memorial Day

Spend the day fasting for world peace. Write a letter to your congressional representatives encouraging peace. Plan a prayer experience or liturgy for peace.

The SPIRITUALITY

# of SUMMER

On early summer mornings there is a coolness as the sun rises over the earth, a prelude of peace before the heat of the day slows the pace across the northern hemisphere. We experience a change in our spirits that calls us to playfulness and new energy. Schoolbooks are put away, classroom doors are closed for the last time. Many of us look forward to a leisure that we do not experience the other nine months of the year. Our spirituality is one of a deep and gentle relaxation in which God plays with us.

Our hearts anticipate the festival of summer life—fruits in abundance, berries and vegetables, summer gardens, picnics and trips to lake and seashore. Summer means a change in momentum. It is not that we do nothing, it is that we begin to do a different work. The work of leisure or the work of play becomes a balm to our souls. Learning to enjoy again the simple things of life and to get in touch with the natural flow of the day is the important lesson of summer.

All the feasts of summer encourage a closeness to nature. We see the world at play, the wonder of ocean waves splashing, the sea life abounding, mountains flowering. We discover anew the dimension of God as playful creator. This change refreshes our souls. It gives us the energy to face again the commitments of work, education, structure and order that will return in the next seasonal cycle.

Summer allows families to bond and grow in ways that might not be possible at any other time. Leisurely afternoons and long evenings when daylight lasts almost until bedtime for little ones create wonderful stretches of time for families to share new experiences. Children come home on those first days of June with a burst of energy, filled with hundreds of ideas for ways to enjoy this break from the academic schedule. Yet any mother can tell you that by August that burst of energy dwindles to intense boredom; the classic wail, "I have nothing to do," is heard on a daily basis. The burden on parents becomes more intense in the summer. Helping children expend their energy in creative ways, looking for teaching moments, finding ways to stimulate children and encourage them to learn in the midst of their more relaxed schedule challenges most of us. This summer section will include many ideas for summer rituals and feasts, for activities that build family life and offer opportunities to rejuvenate our spirits as we play and rest and recreate our own lives in the presence of the Lord.

We seek a summer journey with the Lord, a peaceful time to build our relationship with God. Summer becomes a time of life-giving, fruitful spirituality for every member of the family. Look for the God who knows how to laugh and play, the God who enjoys fresh fruits and walks with you as you watch the summer sun set.

Celebrating Pentecost

C elebrated as the "birthday" of the Church, Pentecost is one of the high points of the liturgical year. But Pentecost has a much older history. It is first a Jewish festival celebrated fifty days after Passover (Deuteronomy 20:1-11). Luke connects the events in the Upper Room with all that has come before. The coming of the Holy Spirit is the climax of Jesus Christ's mission. The Spirit remains with us, as the great gift to the Christian community. Fire and wind are the Spirit's symbols of new life to a weary world. These two symbols vibrate with the pulse of God's presence.

This is a great Sabbath feast. Proclaim a day of rest and play in honor of the Most Holy Playful Spirit. This is Easter's finale. Here are some ways to ring out the last Easter Alleluia.

Play in the Wind ⬖
This is a great day to fly a kite (especially if the ocean or lake shore is near). In keeping with "the spirit" of the day, fly a bird-shaped kite. You may want to build your own and attach a bright Pentecostal-red tail. Fly paper airplanes, blow bubbles in the wind, ride in a convertible, hang a wind chime or a wind catcher. Do something to encounter the wind on Pentecost.

Listen to the Wind ⬖
Play a flute or pennywhistle or wind instrument. If playing a wind instrument is out of your reach, listen to some flute music. The Native American musical tradition is rich with wind music. Borrow a Native American recording from the library and commune with the "Great Spirit" who rides the wind. Enter the music of the spirit in the Gaelic tradition as you listen to Irish flute music.

Visit the Wind ⬖
Go to your favorite windy place. Make a pilgrimage to the lake shore, mountaintop, farm plains, desert vista, oceanside or even the top of a city building, wherever the sound of wind reigns. Read Acts 2:1-11; sing or recite a few verses of "Come, Holy Ghost" or another hymn to the Holy Spirit. Be as still as you can and simply listen to the wind. Ask the Spirit to fall afresh on you!

| Light a Pentecostal Fire | Begin this day as we begin on Holy Saturday. Prepare a bonfire, light a roaring blaze in your fireplace, or simply light a host of candles. Watch the flames dance and entertain you. See the fire anew with a child's eyes. Let the wonder of orange, yellow and red light warm your spirit. Think about what the fire of the Holy Spirit means to you. Pray for someone who is preparing for or recently celebrated Confirmation or pray for the neophytes in your parish. |

| Wear Red | The color red represents the tongues of fire that rested on the heads of Jesus' followers on the day of Pentecost (Acts 2:1-4). In remembrance of the gift of the Holy Spirit wear red on this feast. Invite everyone in your church to put on red as they worship. The "red" congregation will warm everyone's heart. |

| Prepare a Pentecost Meal | On this day when the Church began, prepare a special Sabbath meal. Invite your Confirmation sponsor and godparents. Serve your favorite chili and call it "Flamin' Hot Pentecost Chili." Add to the menu anything that proclaims the day: corn chips and "Spirit" salsa, "fruits of the Spirit" corn muffins. End the meal with flaming cherries jubilee or a birthday cake loaded with candles! |

Celebrating Father's Day

Father's Day is a perfect opportunity to offer a formal expression of love and appreciation to those who gave us life. It is not necessary to spend money on a gift and card, yet it is most necessary to remember our fathers with symbols and words. Try these money-free alternatives to express your honor.

| Interviews About Fathers | Using a cassette recorder, video camera or handwritten card ask a young child questions about Dad's life, such as: "Where does your daddy work?" "How old is your daddy?" "What is your daddy's favorite thing to do?" The answers will delight the unsuspecting dad and be a treasured gift for years to come. |

Prayer for Fathers, Grandfathers and Godfathers:

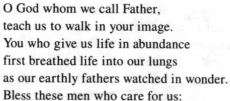

O God whom we call Father,
teach us to walk in your image.
You who give us life in abundance
first breathed life into our lungs
as our earthly fathers watched in wonder.
Bless these men who care for us:
Father, sire, mentor,
men who are made like you.
Give them wisdom and courage.
In their darkest hours may they know your presence.
And may we—those they care for—
honor, respect and reverence them,
keeping their faces in our prayers and hearts for all eternity.
Amen.

The 'Begotten' Game

A favorite method of discussing lineage in the Old Testament is to describe heritage in terms of who begot whom. So, too, for us it is a great method of discovering our roots by doing the same. Ask each family member to start with his or her own name, followed by the name of the father, for example, "Anne, begotten by William, who...." Each person should then tell one interesting fact about his or her father, such as, "has magnificent brown eyes" or "graduated *magna cum laude* from the University of Michigan." Then, the next person does the same about this man who is the father of this family. In the next round, begin with the father and tell about the grandfather. For example, "William, begotten of Stanley, who fought in France during the Second World War." The next round takes it back another generation. Go back as far as you can with the help of older family members.

Celebrating the End of School and Graduation

End-of-School Good-bye Box

With the close of each school year comes a bag of mixed emotions. We are glad to be done with the work of school, yet sad to leave good friends. Bring all these emotions into focus by celebrating the end of the year. Ask each student to put into a box one small object that they will not need till next school year (a pen, a lunch money coin purse, a pencil bag). Each article should have the owner's name on it. Seal the box and write on the top, "Things we will need for the fifth grade" (second, third, fourth and so on). Give the box to next year's teacher for safekeeping. When school begins the next year, the new teacher can meet her students for the first time by opening the box and calling out the name on each article. (For schools with more than one class per grade, these articles may have to be juggled before the beginning of school.)

Good-bye Seeds

Give each student a packet of seeds to grow during the summer. A good choice is sunflower seeds. They grow easily and provide a natural source of food for local birds. Remind students that as their sunflowers grow toward the sun, so should we use the summer as a time of growth and rest.

Major passages in the lives of family members deserve much notice. It is particularly important for young people to be honored when they complete a step in their education. Graduation is a moment to bask in accomplishments and honors. Here are a few ways to do this.

Create-a-Story Graduation Table

Fill a large table with pictures, trophies, mementos of the school years. You may want to include the school colors, yearbook and programs. Provide an autograph book and encourage well-wishers to write a comment or congratulatory message.

Teacher Tales

At least six weeks before graduation, send a short note to some of the graduate's favorite teachers. Ask them to write down memories of this student, a message of encouragement and finally, a commendation to go forward using his or her talents. Include a self-addressed stamped envelope. You may also wish to include letters from coaches, godparents, mentors, pastors and other significant people. Put all the letters in an album along with the graduation program and any special certificates of honor the graduate has earned. This album will be a treasured memento of this well-earned graduation.

The Graduation Gift ⌂

Milestone events present perfect opportunities to give a symbolic gift. The gift becomes a sign of the occasion and a reminder of the grace of the moment. At graduation a perfect gift is a gem. Small semiprecious stones in jewelry, polished rocks, sparkling crystals, make wonderful gifts. These are available at nature stores and other small specialty shops. Accompany this gift with a note that says: "You are a unique gem, a many splendored wonder. Never has there been, or will there be another like you. Your talents, your intelligence, your laughter, your tears are unique. May this gem always remind you of this day and your accomplishments."

Celebrating the Fourth of July

Independence Day is a traditional American day of family, picnics, parades and fireworks. It is the occasion to celebrate all that is good about freedom and rejoice in this bountiful land. Red, white and blue bedeck every storefront, commons and city hall. This secular feast is the occasion of giving thanks to the God "in whom we trust." Pray this prayer as part of your day's festivities.

Freedom Prayer ⌂

Great Spirit of Freedom, Firecracker God,
we play before you today.
This is the feast of grateful memories,
of every woman and man who lived to make us free.
May we never forget our wondrous freedom.
Enkindle in us the red fire of your love
so that no one will ever be denied freedom.
Bless this country in the white hope of honor.
May all we do be cloaked in integrity and honesty.
Pour out upon us the blue grace of humility
that we may serve our world with the bounty of America.
We ask this in the name of Jesus Christ
who lives and reigns in perfect freedom forever. Amen.

Organize a Parade ⌂

Everyone loves a parade, especially children. Gather the children of your neighborhood or church with their bikes, wagons, skates and strollers. Supply plenty of crepe paper, ribbons and balloons. Decorate all the vehicles. Be sure to include a wagon with a portable CD/cassette player loaded with band music and lots of

Sousa marches. Put an adult at the beginning and end of the line and here and there in between. March around the block, down the street or through the town commons. When the parade returns, provide plenty of hot dogs and lemonade to refresh the weary marchers.

'What a State' Picnic
❤

This picnic will help you brush up your geography skills. Invite friends and family to a picnic that features one of the great United States. Display the flag, map and seal of the chosen state. Serve the native foods of that state (for example, Cajun food for Louisiana, Mexican food for Texas, Dutch food for Pennsylvania). Ask everyone to bring one question about this state. Find out the major industry, largest natural resource and other statistics and interesting facts. Whoever answers the most questions correctly takes the state flag home. Each July 4 feature a new state. People will reminisce in future years about the 1990 "Utah" picnic or the 1995 "Hawaii" picnic.

Melting Potluck Supper
❤

America is the place where people from every country come to be free. Discover your neighbors' ancestry by having a neighborhood potluck supper in which each family brings a dish from their ancestral land. This patchwork quilt cuisine will give everyone a taste of what "melting pot" really means.

Celebrating Other Summer Feasts

Rogation Days
❤

In the agricultural world of years past, the Church celebrated "rogation" days before Ascension Thursday. The whole community marched in procession through pasture and field singing the Litany of Saints, asking the Creator, the angels and the saints to bless the crops.

Remember these ancient prayers and do a little planting. Plant a small garden, a strawberry barrel, a tomato plant or even a few petunias in a window box. The mystery of faith is much like sowing and growing. Plant your seeds and read Mark 4:26-34. Then bless your "crops" with this prayer:

> Maker of fruits and flowers,
> bless this work we do.

Creator of fruits and flowers,
kiss the earth and bless our seeds.
May the promise of fertile crops tended by our hands
remind us of your power to bring forth fruit
and your promise to keep those you love in abundance. Amen.

Sacred Heart of Jesus *(Third Friday After Pentecost)*

This is a feast for true lovers. We remember the heart of Christ in a special way. His sacred heart has been the focus of years of Catholic devotion and the special theme of Fridays. The heart of Christ bled to stillness on the cross for the sake of love!

Romans 5:5-11 tells us that this magnificent love is in our hearts too. In honor of the Sacred Heart of Jesus reach out today to the unloved and suffering. Volunteer to clean up a local soup kitchen. At a hospital chapel, pray for those in the building who are suffering and dying that day. Give money to a homeless beggar. Do whatever you think the heart of Christ calls you to do. If the Sacred Heart is to keep beating in our world, we must be the workers of love.

On the evening of this feast watch the sky fill with the red of sunset. Let the sky be your hymn of love to the Sacred Heart. See this quick, silent flash of red light as a reminder that love goes on day in and day out through those who have the courage to beat with the heart of Christ.

June 24
Birth of John the Baptist

We celebrate John's birth on the day when medieval peoples believed that daylight began to decrease. John said, "He [Christ] must increase; I must decrease" (see John 3:30). This summer birthday invites us to be the lamp of the divine light in the spirit of Saint John.

This is a day of fire and water. The desert man, John, knew these signs so well. Fire and water are the lifeblood of a wanderer. Fire warms and gives light in the desert night; water is the source of new life and refreshment in the desert heat. Build a great fire today and splash in your own "Jordan River."

Plan a family picnic near a riverbank, lake shore or seaside. After your meal, build a great fire. See this light as a sacred symbol of God's wonderful love. Take off your shoes and wade in the water. Imagine for a moment that John the Baptizer is with you. Talk to him about the radical choice to follow Jesus. Ask this rebel from the desert to help you walk in the footsteps of Christ. Close with this fire prayer:

Firemaker God, draw us near to you
as we are drawn into these flames.
Thank you for this gracious fire
that invites us to your love,
a blazing reminder of things unseen
but always known deep within our spirits.
Make this fire a vibrant, worthy blaze.
Bless its flames of joy that dance in your love song.
The smoke, too, rises high in praise to you.
O Holy One, we fill our nostrils with the incense of this fire.
Fill us with your Spirit of sweet love, now and forever. Amen.

Create-a-Desert Scene

In honor of John, make a desert scene with your children. If you
have never visited a real desert, this simple project will get you in
touch with the world of the Baptizer. Take a shallow (3") dish and
fill it with sand and just a little dirt. Buy a few small cacti and
place them in your desert pot. Add a rock or two and maybe even
a bone. Put the desert garden in a warm spot and water sparingly
(once a month). Let the little ones touch the prickly cactus skin,
sift through the sand, and rub the rocks and dried old bones.

June 1
**The Day the
Slaves Arrived**

On June 1, 1619, in Virginia the first Negro slaves arrived from
Africa. It marked the beginning of a discrimination that has
plagued America for hundreds of years. Today when you pray at
meals or in the evening remember those who are children of
slavery and discrimination. Ask God to bless and free our country
and world from racial injustice.

June 12
**Saint Anthony's
Vigil**

In Portugal on the eve of the feast of Saint Anthony an annual
festival is held to celebrate the patron of young lovers. It is a night
to honor young love. Tonight, tell the story of your own young
love or perhaps the love story of your parents or grandparents.

June 21
The Summer Solstice

This is the great sun feast and the longest day of the year. It was an ancient day of song, dance and feasting. Rise early and wait for the dawn. Stay outside till the last butter-pink rays fade into night. Celebrate the sun today.

Take a Sunbath

Enjoy a break on a park bench, spread a blanket in the park, go to a city rooftop or wherever the sun shines. Lather on the sun screen and enjoy the warmth of Brother Sun. Read the beautiful "Canticle of Brother Sun" written by Saint Francis of Assisi. Let sunshine invade your soul.

July 14
Bastille Day

Celebrate the French today. Make French toast. Sip a French wine. Wear a beret. Eat brie cheese. Bake a souffle. Go to a French restaurant. Learn a French phrase such as "C'est la vie" or learn to count to twenty in French. Learn to French braid. Rent a French movie. Sing the French national anthem or a French folksong.

July 14
Blessed Kateri Tekakwitha

Native American Catholics each year hold the National Tekakwitha Conference to build bridges between the Catholic tradition and native heritage. In honor of this saint of the Algonquin tribe, find out more about the Tekakwitha Conference by writing to P.O. Box 6759, Great Falls, MT 59401.

Make a Kateri Bracelet

To remember Blessed Kateri Tekakwitha (and entertain the children of summer), make a unique bracelet. String beads or buttons on cord. Use these colors to symbolize the virtues that Kateri practiced: red for the pain of her suffering for Jesus, green for the hope of eternity with God, black for the courage to outstare the darkness, white for the resurrection of Jesus.

July 20
First Moon Landing

On this date in 1969 Neil Armstrong and Edwin Aldrin, Jr., walked on the moon's surface. In their honor, take your own moon walk. After nightfall drive and then walk to a place far from city lights. Find a cozy spot to lay a blanket. Lie back and watch Sister Moon and her friends. After midnight shooting stars will dance across the sky. Look for Vega, Altair and Deneb, the brightest stars. Then try your luck at finding the Big Dipper, the Little Dipper and Sagitarius. When you return home, listen to "Clair de Lune" by Claude Debussy.

July 22
Mary Magdalene
♥

Mary Magdalene was always there. She stayed with Jesus through his death and was the honored one who first encountered the risen Christ. Her steadfast love is the hallmark of Christian courage. An ancient story tells that on the first Easter Sunday Mary Magdalene ran to Pilate's house announcing the resurrection news. Pilate was about to eat a hard-boiled egg as Mary spoke. His retort was that he would believe Jesus had risen from the dead when the egg in his hand turned blood red. In an instant the egg turned red. Pilate at that moment became a believer. Magdalene is often pictured holding a red egg, the first Easter egg. In her honor make "Magdalene Eggs": Place six hard-boiled, peeled eggs in a jar of pickled beet juice. Let marinate at least 4 hours and serve.

July 29
Saint Martha
♥

Martha is the patron of cooks. Celebrate hospitality today. Martha was a "doer" and her sister Mary a "be-er." There is a place for both in the faith community. Martha was a Christian activist in the greatest sense. She would teach us to embrace work as prayer.

In the spirit of Saint Martha arrange a "Martha Exchange" for this day. Find another family willing to share their clutter with you. Designate an area that needs cleaning in each of your houses. Then trade chores! For example, your family goes to your friend's house and cleans their garage while they clean your attic. Perform this task as prayer for the family you serve.

July 30
Birthday of Henry Ford
♥

Henry Ford is the inventor of the first automobile. Plan an adventure in his honor today. Pack a picnic lunch and get into your family car, the great-grandchild of Henry's Model T. Take a day trip to a wonderful little town, state park, historic site or anywhere your heart desires. There's only rule: Do it Henry Ford's style. Use only two-lane roads—no super highways!

August 3
Columbus Sails for New World
♥

Do you have a hard time facing the unknown? In honor of Columbus' courage, why not get lost today? Take the family on a drive on the expressway. Get off at an unknown exit and try to get home using smaller roads and no map. If you are not quite up to high adventure, honor this ancient navigator by making a balloon-powered boat:

Cut away one side of a cardboard milk carton. Cut the end off a bendable straw so the bend is centered between the two ends. Tape one end of the straw inside a balloon. Poke a hole big enough for the straw in the bottom of the carton. Put the balloon inside the carton with the straw protruding through the hole. Bend the straw upwards at a right angle (the propeller) outside the carton. Blow up the balloon and hold the end of the straw. Place in water and let go of the straw. Off she blows!

August 6
The Transfiguration
♥

The summer sun is at its most glorious in the northern hemisphere at this time of year. There is no more fitting time to tell the story of Elijah, Moses and Jesus transformed in radiant glory. We are invited to go to the mountaintop to see God, the law and the prophets. Spend some time in a quiet place with Jesus the Christ today. Adore him. Say nothing. Simply bow in profound reverence before him who is "Light from Light, true God from true God." Read Mark 9:2-10. Then leave your quiet place, your own "holy mountain." As you return to the world, keep his divine presence in your heart.

August 6
Anniversary of Hiroshima
♥

What a horror this day was for the people of Japan. Thousands died, thousands suffered in the end of a hateful war. In the name of those who died, put a single flower on your supper table. Stand around the table before the meal and observe a minute of silent prayer for the victims of the first atomic bomb.

August 10
Saint Lawrence
♥

Lawrence was a deacon who died a martyr when he was grilled to death. He died in 258, yet his example lives on in the lives of countless deacons in today's Church. The permanent diaconate is a viable source of spiritual wealth to us all. If your church has a deacon, or you know one, pick a bouquet of summer flowers and take them to him with a note of thanks.

August 12
Saint Clare
♥

Saint Clare of Assisi followed Francis's footsteps and embraced poverty and simplicity. She began the Order of the Poor Clares. Clare's spirit is still with us today in the lives of thousands of Franciscan sisters and women of the Third Order of Saint Francis. In honor of Clare's call to simplicity and poverty empty your clothes closets today. Give away everything that doesn't fit or that you have not worn in one year. Take your clothing to the nearest St. Vincent de Paul Center or local outlet for the poor. Resolve to live more simply. Ask Clare's advice in those areas of your household and personal life that need trimming.

August 15
The Assumption

Today we celebrate Mary's final journey into heaven. This is a most blessed occasion. There is a sweetness in the air. Mary becomes for all eternity our mother in heaven. We celebrate her purity, her beauty and the wonder of the gift she gave us, Jesus. In many countries this is a harvest festival day. In the middle of August most of the northern hemisphere is bursting with flowers, vegetables and fruit.

Make an Altar

Find a picture or statue of Mary and place it in a prominent place in your home—the family room coffee table, the porch table, the kitchen table, wherever people gather. Place a bouquet of flowers and a small candle in front of your Mary. Before supper, gather together, light your candle and say the Hail Mary.

Visit a Farmer's Market

In Europe this is a harvest festival. Have your own festival. Find a local produce stand, farmers' market or even the produce section of your local grocery. Select a wide variety of fresh fruits and vegetables, then go home and prepare your harvest. Serve up tomatoes, corn, beans, cucumbers, melons and berries. Leave an empty chair at the table and invite the Blessed Mother to join you.

August 27
Saint Monica or 'What a Mother' Day

Monica was the mother of Saint Augustine. It is said that her persistent prayers are responsible for the conversion of this great saint. Who or what do you pray for? Today, spend a little time with your mother, grandmother or godmother. Thank her for all she does for you. Be sure to talk to Saint Monica, too, about all your unanswered prayers.

August 28
Elizabeth Seton's Birthday

Elizabeth Seton, born on this day in 1774, was a strong American woman whose courage and faith brought the gospel to the American Church. She practiced charity as her special concern and founded the religious order of the Sisters of Charity. In Elizabeth's honor perform a few secret acts of love today: Pay the toll for someone behind you at a tollbooth or on the bus, take donuts to your neighborhood fire station, mow your neighbors'

lawn. Go out looking for charity today!

Labor Day

This national holiday of rest is the official end of summer. It is celebrated on the first Monday in September. Say good-bye to summer with a picnic. Decorate with laborers' hats: hard hats, fire hats, nurses' caps, police hats, etc. Ask everyone to answer these questions: When you were eight years old what did you want to be when you grew up? Name all the jobs you have had. If you could work at anything now, what would it be?

The SPIRITUALITY

of FAMILY LIFE

Every family has special days: birthdays, anniversaries, funerals, graduations, adoptions and so on. These feasts are high points of celebration within the family. Each occasion is a moment of grace in which we can proclaim the steadfast love of God. A recent document on family life published by the United States bishops says that our homes and our family units are "the domestic Church." Within the walls of our homes our children first experience the breath of God as we celebrate birthdays, holidays, anniversaries and even funerals. The rhythm of family life teaches that the milestones of our lives together are in the hands of God. Whether we laugh with joy or cry the tears of good-bye, God is with us.

When we create special celebrations to affirm those we love, we speak for God who says you are loved and cared for. Our family feasts will be uniquely our own in the way we celebrate them. These are the moments when the original spirit of each household, each heritage is honored. Here are some ideas you might use to celebrate the comings and goings of your family life.

Celebrating Birthdays

The day of our birth is an anniversary of life. Each year this day stands apart as a moment to reverence our life and the lives of those we love. We should take special care in the way we celebrate. The following are some ways to keep holy this day of life:

Eight Ways to Celebrate Your Day

1. Don't just let the day happen. Plan to do something you enjoy on your birthday.
2. Send flowers to your parents. Thank them for giving you life.
3. Give yourself a gift, something no one knows you would like.
4. Look up on your birth certificate the exact moment of your birth. When that time comes, pause and pray silently for the gift of your life.
5. Donate a book to a school library in your name.
6. Plant a tree for your sake and the sake of the earth.
7. Call on the phone someone from your childhood, perhaps your "best friend" in grade school or a favorite coach or teacher.
8. Take some time off and visit a favorite place: a park, the zoo, a

museum. Take the whole family or go alone, but relax and enjoy your day.

Celebrating on the Half

If a member of your family has a birthday during Christmastime or a child has a summer birthday and never celebrates with schoolmates, consider celebrating a half birthday. Six months after the birthday, have a one-half celebration: Serve a cake that has icing on only one side, give one half of your gift (one sock, one glove, one half of a deck of cards), give one half of a birthday card, blow balloons up only half way, sing the first half of "Happy Birthday to You," take a group photograph of the party goers from the waist down.

Birthday Placemat

What a waste to throw away the notes and cards we receive at birthdays. Create a placemat for a child or elderly birthday person. Create a collage of the cards and interesting facts from the day's newspaper. Arrange them on a piece of construction paper (11" x 16"). Place the paper between two pieces of clear self-adhesive vinyl.

Special Place Setting

To distinguish your birthday person, serve the day's meals on special birthday dinnerware. This place setting should be a unique, one-of-a-kind item. You could purchase a place setting of china, utensils, a glass and napkin in the housewares department of a store or get creative at a thrift store or antique shop. This single table setting is used only on a birthday. This project makes a great gift for someone who lives alone, or as a gift for a family.

Child's Hope Chest

On a child's first birthday give a good-size chest or foot locker. Each year add a gift for their future: a Bible, a dictionary, an antique from a family member, a handmade quilt. The treasures in the chest will become a priceless heritage.

Celebrating Death

Death of a Pet

When a beloved goldfish or an elderly cat finally succumbs to death, it is difficult for children to understand and accept the loss. This occasion is a perfect opportunity to teach children the ritual and process of letting go of someone they love. It is never a good idea to dispose of the animal without any ceremony. This is an occasion for a funeral. Burial can be done with great flourish (or with a great flush, in the case of a goldfish). Gather the family and gently put to rest the family's old friend. Let each family member throw a shovel of dirt into the hole and share a favorite memory of old Buster's or Samantha's life. After the hole is filled say this simple prayer:

God of all creation,
we thank you for the life of_____(pet's name).
He/She was a wonderful companion
and we will miss his/her presence.
Help us to remember the good memories
we have of _____(pet's name).
Please touch our grieving hearts
as we bury our pet.
She/He gave us the gifts of faithfulness and joy.
These gifts will stay in our hearts even as we say good-bye.
Amen.

Find a large rock and a little paint and allow the children to create a tombstone for their lost friend. You may even wish to designate a certain area in your yard as a pet cemetery. During your family's stay in the home, this little corner will be well filled with God's creatures who have accompanied you on life's journey.

Death of a Relative or Friend
❤

The loss of a well-loved elderly relative, particularly a grandparent, can devastate a family. It is not enough simply to acknowledge this passing. It is particularly dangerous not to include children in the funeral. It is important for them to accompany their parents to the services and burial. This is an occasion to proclaim our belief in eternal life.

A simple exercise to help a child grieve is to ask them to write a good-bye letter or draw a picture expressing their memories of and feelings for the deceased person. Let this be personal and private.

Death of a Child
❤

One of the most difficult moments in family life is the loss of a child. Whether through miscarriage, stillbirth or the death of a young family member, the darkness that pervades the lives of the family is overpowering. Siblings have an especially difficult time comprehending the sudden absence of a beloved brother or sister.

So often when a child dies, friends and relatives feel awkward talking about the child's life. Yet nothing consoles a grieving family more than stories about this child. One way to do this is through an album of photographs, remembrances and stories about the child.

Another excellent expression of grief and sympathy is to plant a tree in memory of the child. Flowering or ornamental trees are particularly appropriate; every spring proclaims a beautiful reminder of the precious life. A small plaque could be mounted on the tree, like one a friend found when she moved into a new home: "Danny's Tree." Danny, an infant of the previous owner, died of Sudden Infant Death Syndrome. Every spring as Danny's tree blooms that family prays for Danny and his family.

Visiting the Cemetery ♥

Long after the funeral service is over we may need to confront our loss more privately. A visit to the cemetery can be a therapeutic way to remember and grieve. On Memorial Day many families enjoy the custom of placing flowers on the graves of all of their deceased family members.

Elderly people who no longer drive find it difficult to visit the cemetery. As a wonderful corporal work of mercy you might want to drive an elderly widow or widower to a spouse's grave with a fresh bouquet. Try to remember special occasions when your offer would be most meaningful, such as a wedding anniversary or a spouse's birthday.

Celebrating Anniversaries

In our world the sanctity of marriage needs to be honored, especially on the anniversary of the marriage. Affirming married couples and their holy vocation is an important ministry of the faith community. These are some simple gestures that will affirm couples as they live their vows.

Free Babysitting ♥

Offer to watch a young couple's children at your home. Give the couple an evening free of interruptions in the privacy of their own home. Return the children the next morning with a bouquet of flowers to celebrate the beginning of their next year together.

Periodical Subscription ♡	Send a subscription to a Catholic magazine or newspaper to the couple. The enrichment will continue throughout the year.
Anniversary Care Package ♡	Fill a basket with wine, two glasses, a CD or tape of romantic music, a gourmet cheese and crackers. Include a card or note and place it on the doorstep of the couple.
Memory Album ♡	Older couples enjoy reminiscences about the good old days. Contact friends and relatives who "knew them when" and ask them to share an old photograph and write a memory of a favorite moment from the couple's past. Put your collection in a photo album for the couple to enjoy.

Celebrating Vacations

Vacations can be a blessing or a curse depending on how well prepared you are. Little things can make all the difference. Planning your activities and travel is an important part of your preparation. Here are some simple suggestions that can make this adventure even more fun than you expected.

The Casserole Club ♡	Enlist other families to commit to the Christian concern, "When I was hungry, you gave me to eat." Trade names and vacation dates. On the night your chosen family is returning from their vacation, drop off a prepared casserole supper for them. In turn, when you arrive home, you will be treated to the same luxury.
Travel Journal ♡	Keep a journal of each day of your trip. Include humorous moments, quotes like "At 8:30 A.M., Jason says for the fifth time 'Are we there yet?' " This collection of reflections will be a treasured diary in years to come.

Jelly Roll Pan Desk

For each child in the family prepare a lap desk. Buy a jelly roll pan (it can later be recycled for kitchen use), and fill it with pencil, pen, scissors, crayons, paper, puzzle books, etc. The pan provides a perfect lap desk and the raised edge prevents items from falling off the tray.

The 100-Mile Gift

If you are driving with young children, it is difficult to keep them amused for the long drive. For each 100-mile stretch prepare a small plastic sandwich bag with a surprise in it. As the odometer marks the passing of the 100 miles present the children with a bag. Surprises can include a small toy, a deck of cards or travel game, cookies, sunglasses, etc. This simple plan encourages children to look forward to each milestone and the time passes quickly.

Christmas in July

Plan to purchase or create a vacation Christmas ornament for the family's Christmas tree. Each year look for a little symbol of your vacation, perhaps some miniature replica of something you saw or something distinctive to the area. Attach a hook and the date of the trip and add it to your tree next Christmas.

Vacation Box

Bring an empty box (plain or fancy) on your trip. As you travel fill the box with mementos of the trip: postcards, little souvenirs, match covers, a pretty rock or shell. When you return home, display the box so you can easily revisit your vacation.

Money Buckets

Spending too much on a trip is a common pitfall. In order to conserve and allow children to understand the value of money, prepare a vacation allowance for each child. Decide together what would be an appropriate amount for each "bucket." Take a small container (an empty yogurt cup works well) and give each child this container filled with the allowance. This money is strictly for their souvenirs and special treats.

Color-Coded Fun

Buy everyone on the trip the same color caps or T-shirts. Plan to wear them when visiting crowded tourist spots. It is much easier to find a wandering three-year-old in a bright red cap than a bareheaded child!

Camera Fun

Give each vacationer a disposable camera to chronicle the trip. This gesture will insure plenty of photos of everyone having fun. In addition, you will receive a variety of versions of the same trip.